This one is for your
wondrofwl [...]   !

John

D1380964

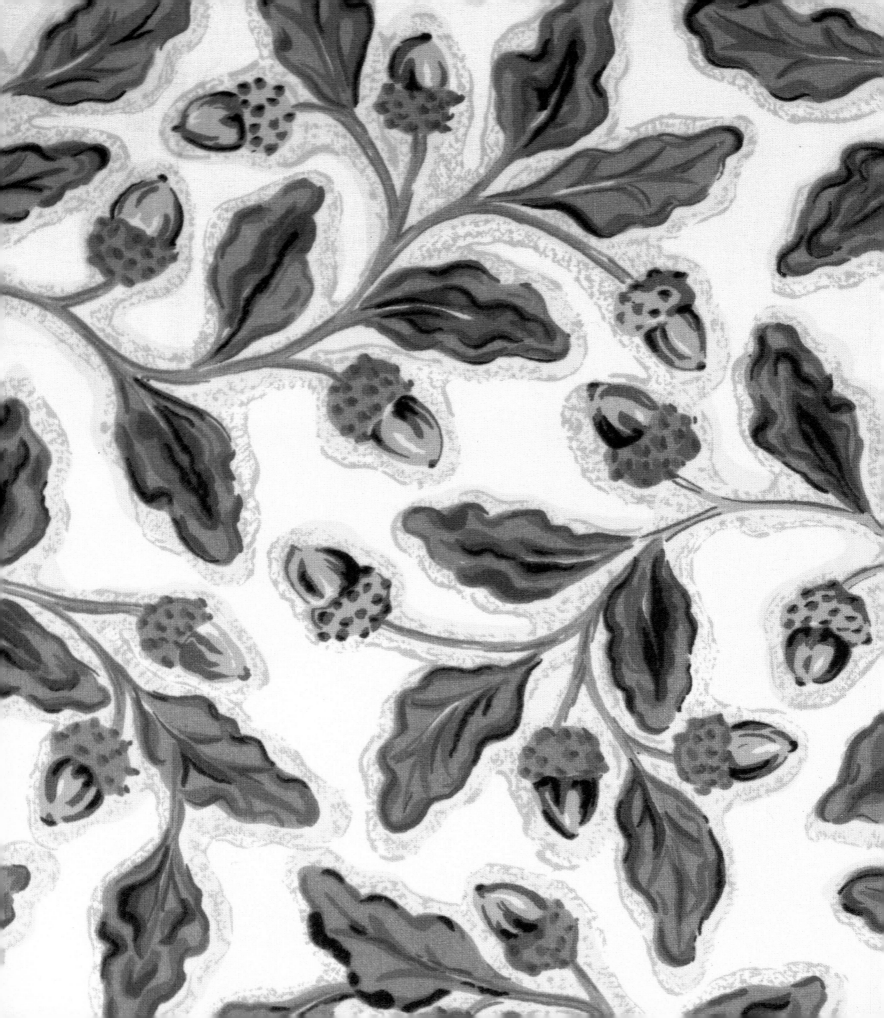

Nina
Campbell

ON
DECORATING

CONRAN OCTOPUS

For my children,
Henrietta, Max and Alice

First published in 1996 by Conran Octopus Limited
37 Shelton Street, London WC2H 9HN

Copyright © Conran Octopus Limited 1996

The fabric/wallpaper designs illustrated on pages 2-5, 8, 24, 42, 52, 66, 74, 88,
96, 108, 116, 132, 142-3, 158 and the endpapers remain the copyright of Nina Campbell.

All rights reserved. No part of this book may be reproduced, stored in a
retrieval system, or transmitted, in any form or by any means, electronic, electrostatic,
magnetic tape, mechanical, photocopying, recording or otherwise, without
prior permission in writing of the Publisher.

COMMISSIONING EDITOR Denny Hemming
PROJECT EDITOR Helen Ridge
ASSISTANT EDITOR Tessa Clayton
ART EDITOR Alison Barclay
PICTURE RESEARCH Julia Pashley
PRODUCTION Mano Mylvaganam

British Library Cataloguing-in-Publication Data
A catalogue record for this book is available from the British Library.
ISBN 1 85029 786 X

Produced by Mandarin Offset Limited
Printed and bound in China

Contents

PREFACE

WHEN CONRAN OCTOPUS APPROACHED ME WITH THE IDEA OF PUBLISHING A BOOK ON MY STYLE OF DECORATING, IT WAS AN INVITATION I COULD NOT REFUSE. HOPEFULLY, IT HAS ENABLED ME TO SHOW, THROUGH THE EXAMPLES OF TEN VERY DIFFERENT COMMISSIONS, THAT THERE IS NO DECORATING PROBLEM THAT CANNOT BE OVERCOME.

DECORATING HAS MUCH MORE TO DO WITH CONFIDENCE THAN TASTE, AND CERTAINLY SHOULDN'T BE DEPENDENT ON PREVAILING FASHIONS. IT'S IMPORTANT TO FOLLOW YOUR HEART, AND YOUR EYE. AFTER ALL, IT'S YOUR HOME THAT YOU ARE DECORATING AND YOU MUST BE HAPPY LIVING WITH THE RESULTS. DECORATING RULES, LIKE ANY RULES, ARE MEANT TO BE BROKEN – I BREAK THEM ALL THE TIME.

I WOULD LIKE TO THANK ALL MY CLIENTS WHO SO KINDLY AGREED TO HAVE THEIR HOMES PUT ON DISPLAY. WITHOUT THEIR COOPERATION AND GENEROSITY, THIS BOOK WOULD NOT HAVE BEEN POSSIBLE.

Nina Campbell

CHAPTER 1

Nina Campbell

HER DECORATING ETHOS

Nina Campbell has been designing and decorating stylish interiors for over thirty years. Her skill and expertise have earned her an impressive list of clients, and her work regularly takes her all over the world. She lives and works in London and has a small shop, with offices above, in a quiet street situated just behind Harrods.

Why did she become a designer?

ABOVE AND FAR RIGHT: The stylish interiors of John Fowler, including this drawing-room and bedroom designed with Nancy Lancaster, were a great influence during my early years. The French armchair in the bedroom is covered in 'Berkeley Sprig', a design inspired by a scrap of antique wallpaper that John found whilst renovating a property in London's Berkeley Square. Years later I redecorated the entrance to Annabel's Club, situated in the basement of the same building. I asked John if the paper could be reproduced for its decoration. He agreed, and 'Berkeley Sprig' has been a signature of Colefax & Fowler ever since.

probably became a designer because I was incapable of doing anything else. My early life – I was born on the last day of World War II – was spent moving from one house to another, as my parents were inveterate movers. When there was no one to play with, I accompanied my mother to Coles in Mortimer Street to choose wallpaper for my next bedroom. This was a chore I never tired of and one that undoubtedly helped to shape my life.

My passion for houses and decoration developed despite the scarcity of post-war fabrics. Both my parents had wonderful taste and were immensely inventive. My mother bought a bolt of taffeta at a warehouse sale and dyed it acid yellow for our drawing-room curtains, which we transported from house to house. (Our drawing-rooms always had pale blue walls to complement them, while a pair of tapestry-covered chairs formed the nucleus of each room.) The staircase in each house was covered with a runner made of thick, dark green art felt and secured by brass stair rods. The carpet was brushed every day, and the stair rods were polished by hand. Hard work, but a brilliant effect.

Helping to move furniture about became part of my upbringing. When I was about twelve I'd sit up with my mother after dinner and we'd have the urge to rearrange the furniture. Needless to say, halfway through we'd get tired and go to bed, leaving sofas and chairs on the landing or halfway up the staircase.

My first job was in the gift department of The General Trading Company in Chelsea, which I thoroughly enjoyed and which probably whetted my appetite for having a shop of my own. After a short break learning shorthand and typing, I returned to The General Trading Company to run their wedding list department, a fantastic job which entailed learning about all the other departments in this fascinating store and then translating them into other people's lives.

I left after about eighteen months, having been offered a trip to America to visit my grandmother, see New York and spend a month in Jamaica – irresistible at the age of eighteen. On my return, I was interviewed by John Fowler for a job as his assistant at Colefax & Fowler. He was distinctly unimpressed on learning that I had completed a design and architecture course, saying, 'Forget everything you've been taught, child, because you clearly know nothing! But why not start next week?' I became his official bag-carrier, undertaking menial tasks with the greatest pleasure. He had no idea how half-witted I was. I was far too busy 'doing the season' and having a whale of a time, but I loved the job and worked extremely hard. I soon learned that John's knowledge of design and decoration was positively encyclopaedic and I couldn't help but learn.

Although quite a taskmaster, John was deeply loved by all. I remember nervously asking if I could leave two hours early on a Friday to go to a ball at Chatsworth, Derbyshire, home of the Duke and Duchess of Devonshire. 'Darling child,' he

replied, 'you must leave on Thursday, but make sure you don't spend all your time dancing. You must look at ...' And then followed a list of pictures, furniture and so on, and, of course, close questioning about my intended dress, hairstyle and jewellery.

After a couple of years with the company, I was given the go-ahead to decorate the odd room on my own. John was re-decorating the public apartments of a stately home and I was asked to work on the private apartments, as a cost-saving measure. That was the greatest fun because it meant raiding attics, finding furniture in a sorry state and restoring it to its former glory. Some of the rooms I decorated hadn't been touched for years.

I was on my way.

At twenty-two, I left Colefax & Fowler and set up my own decorating business with a friend, a former client. One of my first commissions was to decorate Cullen House in Banffshire, Scotland. This marathon task took over four years to complete. Years later the house was sold and the family moved into the dower house, which I had previously decorated as a sporting lodge. We moved their furniture and possessions over from the main house and made them work equally well in their new home. It is very rewarding to be asked back by clients when it's time for them to move and to reorganize them in a different setting.

Another exciting commission was helping with the decoration of Dudmaston House in Shropshire. Already full of wonderful possessions, including porcelain, watercolours, and so on, the house really only needed 'background'. Nowadays, with more and more people buying second and third homes, and not always having the necessary pieces of furniture, the decorator is often asked to find those as well – quite another matter.

I was learning from the masters – and from others, too. For example, I was asked to decorate a magnificent town house. The owner, the most elegant woman I have ever worked for, had a splendid collection of modern paintings, coupled with beautiful eighteenth-century furniture, for which she needed a calm background. The result – a successful juxtaposition of antique and modern – was unlike anything else I had previously done and gave me plenty of inspiration for future decorative schemes.

For a few months my business partner and I worked from the basement of her London apartment, with everything going swimmingly until the landlord became aware of pieces of furniture and bales of fabric stacked in the corridor. He pointed out that the lease was residential and suggested we find other, more appropriate, premises from which to conduct our business. At this point, I took a space in the building of a London firm of architects. It was the ideal working environment: under one roof there were architects, surveyors and garden designers, along with a superb reference library.

ABOVE: Mark Birley and I designed this sitting-room in the 1970s for his newly acquired Mark's Club in Mayfair. We chose a Fortuny fabric for the walls, and found a wonderful pair of mahogany doors and a fireplace to give the room a sense of scale.

When my partner eventually left the business to live abroad, I decided to pursue my other 'hankering' and set up shop with Mark Birley (then owner of Annabel's Club) in Pimlico. Here we marketed 'unashamed luxury': the finest linens from Porthault, cushions made from exotic antique batik, bamboo bath racks, even boiled sweets from Fauchon in Paris. But, eventually, my passion for design and decoration resurfaced. Meanwhile, Mark had bought a club, Mark's Club, in Mayfair and asked me to decorate it with him. Working with such a perfectionist was a tremendously exciting and rewarding experience.

The Pimlico shop inevitably proved too small, and, as I found myself more and more involved in decorating, Mark and I decided to part company. I took on a shop at No. 48 Walton Street, Chelsea. Eventually I needed No. 54 as well, and then a whole building, opposite at number 9, came on the market. On that day I was lunching with a close friend who had at one time run a business from that address, which I took for a good omen. I made an offer for the premises, and we are still there today, albeit rather cramped.

Before too long I started printing my own fabrics. It all began with a little criss-cross material from Tissunique, which I needed for a job in Scotland. Sadly, the fabric was discontinued but I obtained permission to reprint it. That was the beginning of my fabric collection, which soon included myriad rose-patterned chintzes and trellis-motif designs based on old documents and shawls from Alsace. It was all rather alarming. Suddenly the business began to develop into something very serious, taking me with it!

Although I design fabrics, I still consider myself, first and foremost, an interior designer, and because of that I look at fabric design from a different point of view. When creating my two annual collections of fabrics and wallpapers, which are distributed through Osborne & Little, I always try to think how these fabrics will be used, and with what. Because I use the same colour palettes year after year, if a customer wishes to change her drawing-room curtains but does not want to redecorate the whole room, she can. There will always be something new to go with an old favourite.

Apart from John Fowler and Mark Birley, one other person had a decisive, although more distant, influence on my career: Elsie de Wolfe, the legendary American decorator, whose career spanned almost fifty years from the turn of the century. What fascinated me most about her was the fact that she virtually fell into the job of decorator. She was the first professional interior designer, and certainly the first to practise self-promotion in a big way. She was an adventuress and tried things long before anybody else. She used leopard-skin in innovative ways and wherever she could, and mirrored everything that stood still. On top of all that she was among the first of the latter-day New York property developers.

ABOVE: The famous fern design in green and white, much favoured by Elsie de Wolfe and a personal favourite of mine.

MY APPROACH TO DECORATION

When I am first consulted about a commission, I try to find out everything I can about my prospective clients. How do they live and how do they think they want to live? What do they like? How do they entertain? How do they spend their weekends? How many children live at home? (Children should be included at the planning stage; after all, it's their home too.) I find out all I can and then, so to speak, give them the canvas on which they can paint or repaint their lives.

When you take on a commission, you are beginning a personal relationship that needs to work. Sometimes it goes like a dream. I once decorated an apartment for a couple who were dotty about cars and motorbikes. I became so immersed in the job and entranced by their passion that I ended up designing their garage and advising them on what they should wear on the motorbike!

Once a relationship has been established, the next step is the budget. I believe in extensive discussion and all-inclusive estimates, so that everyone concerned knows exactly where they stand. We can then, if necessary, add, cut down, or find alternative ways of doing things.

But what if you are designing and decorating on your own account? In the words of Elsie de Wolfe, suitability and practicality are the first considerations. Start with those and you can't go far wrong. Think about interior decoration in the same way as you think about clothes – a dance dress isn't ideal for a walk in the country, and a white carpet in a country drawing-room, with French windows opening onto a garden, is likely to be in a sorry state after a long, wet winter.

Before decorating either a house or just one room, you must first decide what you want from it and how you wish it to work. Make sure that each room has an affinity with the surrounding rooms or passageways so that it doesn't come as a visual shock to visitors – or even to you – on entry. A house works much better if one space flows into another.

When it comes to the fabrics required for a commission, I prefer not to mention price as this is apt to cloud judgement. Far better to say nothing. Then, if my clients do fall for something outrageously expensive, I will do my best to massage the budget and work it into the scheme – so often it's the expensive fabric that pulls a scheme together. However, if the fabric proves to be too costly, I might try using it in moderation, which can be just as effective. I recall a client falling hopelessly in love with a ruinously expensive print which she wanted for her drawing-room curtains. With a little persuasion, she agreed to use the print for a pair of French chairs instead, and we made very stylish curtains using two inexpensive, plain-coloured fabrics. The chairs, however, remained the decorative heart of the matter. Such compromises can be made to work to your advantage when decorating your *own* home.

FAR LEFT: Originally a Presbyterian church, London's Belfrey Club had a high-vaulted ceiling which looked rather cold and bleak, and there was no way to curtain the rather awkwardly shaped windows. I therefore commissioned a painted fantasy skyscape in midnight blue fading to pale blue, covered with stars, birds and butterflies.

ABOVE: Mixing fabrics and wall coverings of different patterns and colours can be extremely effective. Checks, stripes and bold floral designs in shades of grey, yellow and lavender create an overall effect that is restful and not at all busy.

Don't despair about reusing old things – and I don't just mean furniture – from a previous home. Having such items around you can prove very comforting; after all, they're old friends, so change the way you use them instead. My last house had low ceilings while those in my present apartment are much higher. I wanted to re-create the look of my old bedroom using the same bed drapery, so I removed the pelmet and used the fabric to lengthen the curtains, thus creating a plain top and huge frill at the base. These touches of continuity are important whether you are moving into a new house or simply redecorating; your home should remain your home, albeit revamped and improved.

Proportion, too, is a fundamental principle of decorating. I've always found it better to err on the generous side when provided with a choice: large cushions rather than small; deep fringes rather than shallow, and so on. Rules are there to be broken, of course, but decorating is rarely improved by substituting the small and safe for the grand and generous – as in personality, so in decoration.

Scale is a very important part of this equation. Mixing large-scale and small-scale usually works well, whereas combining middle- and small-scale is seldom successful. Sometimes two medium-scale patterns can work together if the colour palette is reversed. Throw in stripes, checks and plaids to balance the large and smaller designs, and use patterns judiciously, paying attention to *where* you use them. Don't lose your nerve and, above all, don't ask your friends for their opinion. And finally (but, oddly enough, also primarily), never forget the worth of good, plain colours and mixing textures.

Developing your own style

Style evolves with experience. Don't be too self-conscious or impulsive when developing your own style. It will happen. I am told that I have a style that makes people feel at ease. First-time visitors to my home might expect it to be rather intimidating. Yet, everyone always remarks on how relaxed they feel. Rooms are for living in. Life is stressful enough without living in a showroom.

Since I am blissfully unfettered by formal training, I have few rules. For example, if one piece of furniture works with another, then I'm not going to worry about what periods they're from. What pleases is what counts.

I like a classic look that doesn't date, but there are certain elements, such as the shape of a lampshade, that need to be updated from time to time. I have clients whose rooms haven't changed for years and they still look wonderful. (In a strange way, a room needs time to settle into itself and is often better a few weeks after it has been finished, so don't pass judgement on your efforts too soon.)

In my opinion the key to good decorating is most definitely comfort: comfort combined with colours that blend.

*T*HAT ELUSIVE MATTER OF LIGHT

I have long enjoyed natural light coming through unlined curtains. Huge windows, however, are apt to accentuate grey days and black skies, so make allowances for these natural misdemeanours. You need to be able to draw curtains, especially with the approach of dark evenings. One solution I have used successfully is to have a pair of curtains framing the window with undercurtains that can be drawn at night.

Overhead lighting has earned itself a bad name. Yet there are places where a chandelier is perfect – in the dining-room, for example – but not with a blaze of downward light. Candlelight is lovely, especially in the drawing-room after dinner, and rooms lit by candles take on a wonderfully romantic glow.

Table lamps provide most of my lighting – there's nothing nicer than soft pools of light dotted about a room. Reading lights, however, are quite another matter. They should be carefully considered and strategically placed with the light directed down on book, newspaper or magazine.

ABOVE: We keep photographs and paintings of family and friends, so why not of our homes, past and present? Marianne Topham's watercolour brilliantly captures the elegance and comfort of my drawing-room on a sunny day.

ABOVE: *A brass library light attached to a bookcase is an ideal solution if you are short of shelf space for a lamp.*

RIGHT: *With daylight obscured by trees just outside the window, this library was dark and gloomy. Rather than try to make the room appear lighter, I chose to make it darker, and consequently warmer and more inviting, using deep, rich colours – olive green on the wooden panelling and green and claret linen curtains.*

A particularly important point is the balance of light. Only recently I decorated a barn with the help of a professional lighting firm because table lamps were not going to achieve the desired effect. We needed a versatile lighting scheme with spotlights highlighting the beams. It's important to know when to bring in the professionals and when not. There are many beautiful lights on the market but it's imperative to put them where they're appropriate.

The importance of colour

Don't be afraid of colour and be sure to use colour with depth. For instance, it is important to remember that you can't necessarily make a dark and dingy room light by using pale colours. You will just make it duller. In fact, it's better to forget about that quest for a light room. Far better to opt for strong, dark, jewel-like colours that make it vibrant. Making a dark room darker will create a feeling of comfort, warmth and richness.

Conversely, if you have a room with large windows that is flooded with natural light, make it lighter. Remember, too, that light rooms can drain colour, so in these circumstances it is far better to use paler, cooler colours. The results will both astonish and delight. A rich range of decorative effects can be achieved without using any colour at all – off-white decorating is the perfect foil in rooms that look out onto terraces and gardens.

The effects of daylight and artificial light on a room are very different, and how your room appears at different times of the day needs careful study before you choose your colour scheme.

You can use colour inexpensively yet to advantage in, say, a dining-room. Change the look by using different slip-covers on the chairs and by your choice of china, glass and candles. Similarly, introduce changes of colour in a bathroom with towels or in a bedroom with bed linen. To reflect the changing seasons and completely alter the feel of a room, you can put pale cotton loose covers over rich velvet or

LEFT: *This bedroom is fortunate to have natural light streaming in through the windows at each end of the room. To make the room even lighter, I used a very pale wallpaper in colours that complement the attractive auricula-patterned chintz of the bed drapery and curtains. As there were no architectural details to speak of, I added a wallpaper border to define the contours of the room.*

tartan upholstery. Your room needs to be brighter in winter than in summer, and during the day far more than at night. You can carry out such colour experiments for a surprisingly modest cost.

Over-zealous colour matching can often prove an expensive mistake. You need to step back, even leave the room from time to time, and consider the overall scheme. Then choose something slightly 'off' the main colour you had in mind. It is likely to prove more relaxed, less contrived and easier to live with.

Versatility in design and decoration

Versatility is important in rooms lacking space – or rooms used for more than one purpose. Dining-rooms, for instance, can verge on the dull, so why not create a library-cum-dining-room? Nothing is more pleasant than eating surrounded by books. Then there are conservatory-dining-rooms. These can be the most spectacular dual-purpose rooms in the house, and the most flexible. My own incorporates the laundry room!

Some people even like to combine bedroom and bathroom, but as Elsie de Wolfe commanded so dictatorially: 'Keep unmentionables out of the way!' At the other end of the scale, it's a real treat to have a large bedroom, complete with roaring fire, comfortable sofa, television and telephone, with an equally warm bathroom just next door – truly en suite.

Studies make good spare bedrooms, as long as you have a cupboard or closet. It's so tiresome as a guest to have to leave your clothes in the suitcase because there's nowhere else to put them. Such a room becomes an overnight hovel. Storage is important everywhere, of course. Tidy cupboards make life easier and more organized, and no chatelaine ever had too many cupboards.

It's always worthwhile spending time, preferably ensconced in an armchair, figuring out how to make your living space even more comfortable, whether for yourself, your children or your guests. If things are done well, there will be no need to redo them.

FAR RIGHT: As there was no en suite bathroom, a previous generation of owners had put in the marvellous basin in this country-house bedroom. The only addition I needed to make was the folding screen to shield the fireside chair from the plumbing.

Wit and humour

A touch of humour or wit (contrary to popular opinion, they are actually very different) can be most effective but must be subtly introduced, adding just that element of surprise or double-take.

Mirrors can be witty if they're strategically placed between the windows with pictures or lights fixed onto them. A folding screen, which has been given a highly personal touch, can prove an even more engrossing object of general interest. Peter Coats, the eminent gardener, possessed a screen that was also a pictorial record of his gardening career.

ABOVE: *This trompe l'oeil design was a decorative indulgence on my part. Featuring a tureen with Taurus the bull, my star sign, on top of the lid, it 'hangs' on my kitchen wall alongside a collection of blue and white china plates, both real and trompe l'oeil.*

A decorated dining-table can also provide entertainment and help to break the ice when the conversation is slow to get started. You can do so many amusing and inventive things. On one occasion, while the builders were at work in the house, a talented friend gave a big lunch party in my chaotic apartment. We covered the table with newspaper, made a centre-piece with tiny paint pots and brushes, used toy builder's hard hats with names painted on them as place cards, and a dustpan lined with silver foil as a cheese platter.

My daughter Henrietta's twenty-first birthday party took place on the roof terrace in July and was dominated by hot colours: hot pink, acid yellow, lime green and bright orange gerberas in single stemmed vases all over the tables, with yellow and pink paper napkins and candles. Fun and young. The important thing to remember is never be left with an aftermath: these indulgences are essentially temporary – and disposable. Here today and certainly gone tomorrow.

An unusual, out-of-scale object – obelisk, vase, statue or whatever – can add interest for its own sake; and *trompe l'oeil* can be a source of immense fun and discussion. Wit can be prompted by thrift: pictures cut from magazines and framed can look every bit as effective as a genuine and far more expensive print or etching. If you collect something out of the ordinary – take my passion for monkeys, for example – it can bring amusement to a decorative scheme, initially for you, then for others, too.

Finishing touches

Finishing touches should be precisely that. But don't indulge in them when you're just starting on a room. John Fowler always said, 'Make sure you've got an escape-hatch somewhere near the end of the job.' A room decorated using a somewhat austere blueprint can be bland and needs a flash of inspiration to pull it together, but don't leave it too late, either; if you've completed everything, it may not be possible.

Personal possessions – whether match-strikers, bronzes or collections of porcelain – are very important and can prove the most delightful of all finishing touches, such as the tiny pillow, made by Henrietta, that says 'A good mother needs lots and lots of love.'

Cushions, rugs, lamps and ornaments are last-minute things. I'm not suggesting that rooms should be left to drag on and on for months. Far from it. But most rooms need decorative additions once the job is done. You may need to acquire something extra. Mirrors are an essential ingredient – they trick the eye and you can, with candles, create a sense of glamour in virtually any room.

Remember to edit: if there is a lot of clutter lying around, it will need frequent and ruthless sorting-out. Before I start to hang pictures or place objects I lay everything out in front of me, take stock and then get rid of what is superfluous.

A friend recently said to me, 'I've too much blue and white china. What shall I do, Nina? You're the expert.' 'Not at all,' I replied, 'but why not select the best pieces and say goodbye to the rest?' And that is exactly what she did, and to her advantage. Motley collections can so easily take over a room, even a house, so, although it's not always that easy, try not to become too attached to too many things. It will make the editing less painful.

PAINTERS AND DECORATORS

Working with painters and decorators is where wit and humour are certainly needed, although I'm fortunate in that I usually work with the same people.

Good builders, working in harmony, can create an aura of calm which in turn underpins the ultimate success of the whole project, especially if major structural changes are involved. If things do go wrong, all you can say is: 'Listen, we've made a mistake and we have to put it right.'

Then there are the irreplaceable specialists. For me, the artist responsible for creating special effects or *trompe l'oeil* treatments is a particularly valuable team player. I never have problems in this sphere, as I can always contact an unusually talented specialist I've known and commissioned throughout my working life. I like to use people I know. It's not that I'm averse to others, but if you come to know and respect professionals' talents, you are on the way to creating good team spirit, which is essential to any job.

Large-scale jobs should be run by an architect and overseen by a foreman. On our most successful jobs we have always had a good foreman – basically he's there to prevent the bill soaring sky-high. And in this area you need to be very disciplined on your own account. It's the easiest thing in the world to ask your painter to take the dog for a walk or pick up the cleaning on his way in to work and then wonder why the bill has escalated so alarmingly. Specialists should be doing specialist jobs – at, alas, their specialist rates!

So much for the basic practicalities of decoration. Once you have these sorted out, the rest should be sheer entertainment.

CHAPTER 2

CLASSIC ENGLISH STYLE

Nina's unusual home comprises two floors of three late nineteenth-century terraced houses. Situated in central London, the spacious apartment has given Nina what she desired above all else: an enfilade of magnificent reception rooms and a light, airy conservatory.

Obtaining permission to proceed with the alterations necessary for the building conversion proved a drawn-out and tedious task, but, after what seemed an extremely long year to Nina, her plans were finally approved.

Moving from a house, which was considered the perfect base for the family, to an apartment, however spacious, was likely to arouse some dissent, so Nina took care to discuss with all the members of her family every possible means of making them feel at ease with their new living space. After all, a home needs to be a place where children can grow up comfortably, at first with their toys and then with their ever-growing personal paraphernalia, ranging from books to personal computers.

The current layout is flexible enough to cope with the full and varied lives of both Nina and her children. The aim was to provide five bedrooms, four bathrooms, a drawing-room, library, kitchen and conservatory. Before any alterations took place, however, adequate time was spent working out the overall plan.

For Nina, this stage of the proceedings is, in many ways, the most imperative part of any scheme. Everyone's views, however self-indulgent they may seem, must be considered at an early stage. Then the necessary structural alterations can follow, while ensuring that due consideration is given to authentic period features, such as cornices and ceiling decoration. These enrichments provide valuable visual interest and can transform an undistinguished room into somewhere very special.

Decoration should always evolve to suit your own tastes and needs

ENTRANCE HALL

My first challenge was the minute entrance hall, which resembled nothing more than a dark box with a flat roof, with a recessed light that fitted so badly our family conversations could be heard clearly in the apartment upstairs. I decided to capture something of the mood and mystique of a forest. Don't ask me why; it was something I had always dreamed of. I started by creating a green crackle-glazed effect on the walls, doors and ceiling, achieved by mixing water-based paint and oil glaze, and then decorating the surfaces with a gilt leaf design. The most imaginative touch – and a decorative triumph as far as I was concerned – was the tiny, mirror-backed glass cupola that was slotted into the restricted roof space and now illuminates the entrance hall with what I call 'distilled daylight'.

AN ENFILADE OF RECEPTION ROOMS

The generous proportions of the reception rooms establish a feeling of spaciousness which is echoed throughout the apartment. Imposing double doors lead into our drawing-room and library beyond. (Incidentally, handsome as they are, they are also fire doors.)

Whether the reception rooms are used for sophisticated evenings or their more usual relaxed role, comfort is my key word. On formal occasions, few things can be more irritating than sitting on a sofa and worrying about creasing the covers or crumpling the cushions. It is important that guests feel at their ease. At other times, when we are on our own, we should be able to relax in peace and tranquillity after a hard day's work.

Left: The drawing-room in its earliest incarnation. The furniture arrangement was later changed to create more seating space for larger parties. Right: The entrance door to the apartment, decorated with a wonderful green crackle-glazed finish and tendrils of gilt leaves.

ᴅRAWING-ROOM

As the drawing-room is always the first room that visitors see, let us start there. The room's modest grandeur is exemplified by the fireplace – a grand white marble Victorian piece – which was already in place. A sense of continuity was readily established by moving an almost identical chimney-piece from one of the bedrooms into the library beyond. This gave the two rooms a splendid unity, as well as providing a great space for larger parties. On these occasions, the solid wooden doors, which replaced inappropriate folding doors, really prove their worth, allowing the rooms their separate identities, but also opening up the whole area for special events.

Versatility is an important factor in the drawing-room. For large dinner parties, most of the furniture is taken out of the room, creating space for two tables of eight, which can be decorated with a riot of colourful table linen and bouquets of fresh flowers.

The high ceiling and the generous proportions of the drawing-room partly dictated the style of its decoration. No architectural embellishments were necessary, except for a dado rail, which helps break up the impressive wall space.

Left: As the drawing-room leads directly into the library, I chose to link the rooms by using lighter shades of colour in the drawing-room and deepening them in the library.

Right: In the most recent drawing-room arrangement, the large upholstered ottoman creates the ideal room-break as well as offering the perfect seating solution for larger parties: guests sitting on it can face whichever direction they choose, allowing seating at both ends of the room to be used at the same time.

I have a fondness for huge family portraits which line the walls to the same end result. Comfortable sofas and chairs are grouped around the fireplace, giving the room an intimate, country-house feel. Comfort by day and glamour by night was the scheme I was looking for.

The decoration of your home should always evolve to suit your own tastes and needs and those of your family, and certainly not look as if it has come straight out of a decorating textbook or magazine. Colours must flow, one into the other, and not look jumpy. In my apartment, the proximity of the library to the drawing-room established the importance of using colours that would harmonize with each other and continue the sense of unity from one room to the next. Hence, I chose a scheme based on shades of creamy beige, with beige linen damask – a looser interpretation of silk damask, which seemed too formal – echoing the beige and stone striped linen on the library walls. I am particularly fond of beige and use it often because it is the most wonderful colour for underpinning and playing up the richness of more vibrant tones. 'Ploys on beige' may sound basic, but it works like a dream.

Be bold with your decoration, mix different textures and patterns, but avoid too many different combinations as this will result in a very busy background. I have used a variety of textures and patterns throughout the room, but with variations in scale. A balance of larger and smaller patterns is more pleasing to look at than too many of the same size. Injections of colour can be added at a later stage with cushions and fresh flowers. The main objective is to make the whole decorative scheme look as if it has been casually created and not intellectually contrived.

Linking adjoining rooms to one another by the harmonious use of colour promotes both a feeling of calm and unity as well as pleasing the eye

Textured and plain fabrics work well together, but a sound guideline to follow is 'avoid using too many stripes'. Although attractive, geometric patterns can soon get on each other's nerves, and conflicts in decoration spell disaster. A cushion with a strip of tapestry on it and striped curtains will normally work well together, but they must be what I term 'first cousins' or 'near neighbours'. In the drawing-room I mixed together a variety of different textures, including needlework, silk, cotton, velvet, damask, wool, mohair and tapestry. Although there is plenty of visual interest, the end result doesn't appear hectic or overwhelming. Nothing is worse than walking into a room and thinking your head is going to explode.

The windows are dressed with an elaborate curtain treatment using the same fabric as that used for the walls – there really is nothing to compare with the effect of sumptuous drapery. More often than not, though, the pretty, unlined striped undercurtains are drawn instead of the heavy top curtains for a lighter, less claustrophobic atmosphere.

The space between the windows was mirrored, then framed with a gilt strip and hung with paintings – a dash of visual trickery to create an impression of depth. Mirror adds sparkle and sparkle equals glamour. I used red, black and touches of gilt to create a truly wonderful richness, and candlelight reflected in the mirror at night is a joy.

I have used soft background lighting throughout the drawing-room. Lighting is, I think, a most important element, especially in a northern climate with its dark autumn and winter evenings, but one that is too often neglected. First of all, you must determine the quantity and quality of light you require, and then look for the type of

Left: The reflections in this glamorous gilt-framed mirror fixed between the drawing-room windows tantalize the eye and create an air of mystery. The room is glimpsed in its summer guise, with cool white sofa covers over the patterned upholstery.

To a certain degree, the size and scale of my drawing-room dictated the seating arrangement, allowing different areas to be implied rather than defined, thus avoiding dividing the room too decisively. However, I wanted to be able to accommodate at least six people around the fireplace – something of a problem even in the largest of rooms. At one stage, a sizeable three-seater sofa with a desk behind held the centre of the room, with two big comfortable armchairs placed either side of the fireplace. Although an imposing arrangement, it was, nevertheless, impractical. Trial and error proved that the solution was to add a club fender, with a sofa positioned either side of the fireplace, and place the armchairs at the far end of the room – a practical as well as decorative arrangement.

Paintings play a significant role in the decoration of any room. Many people group paintings and prints according to subject or texture. This can work quite well, but such an arrangement may look too rigid and resemble an art gallery. Hang your paintings in a way that you find pleasurable. Be confident and self-assured; in my case I have hung, somewhat tongue-in-cheek, grand ancestral portraits next to light-hearted paintings of monkeys at play. At one end of the room there is a floor-to-ceiling portrait of the children's great-grandmother by Sir John Lavery. This has proved the perfect backdrop for a pair of Edwardian chairs, decorated with needlework panels taken from a pair of antique curtains, and has certainly not overpowered near neighbours, even quite small paintings.

Personal possessions, for example, photographs, tortoiseshell curios, bronzes and family memorabilia, should be given due prominence. They can be grouped informally, although with some sense of order, on table tops and the mantelpiece. Personal belongings are all expressions of your personality, as indeed a room should be, and are the elements that make a room come alive.

fitting that suits the style of the room. In this instance, I have used a combination of stylish gilt wall sconces, converted altar candlesticks and large antique tea caddies, in conjunction with candles. Although lighting is the trickiest of all decorative problems, it is certainly the most rewarding once you've found the answers.

And what about that other basic need: furniture? When arranging your furniture, try putting everything you own where you think it should go, then begin to weed out those pieces that look out of place. And always try pieces that you are unsure about. It may be that the large chest you always thought so intimidating will make a tiny room appear bigger than it really is, whereas lots of small tables may accentuate unduly the modest size of a tiny room. Above all, you have to feel comfortable with your furniture. A home should always evolve around its occupants, certainly not the other way round.

Above: Sofas, positioned either side of the fireplace, and a club fender can seat six people in comfort around the fire.
Right: The boldly patterned print on this circular table cloth brings together all the colours used throughout the drawing-room, and is a perfect backdrop for a collection of tortoiseshell curios.

ℒIBRARY

The library is also used as a second drawing-room and doubles-up as a dining-room whenever we have a large dinner party. However, my aim right from the beginning was to create an informal, yet flexible, family room, where the children could put their feet on the sofa without getting

into trouble. To this end, the decoration had to be both practical and simple; anything too elaborate or busy would have been completely inappropriate. Hence my choice of dark colours for the upholstery, heavy linen curtains and a practical, patterned carpet.

Grouped around the fireplace are old nursery chairs, covered in a red tartan. The most individual and often most useful addition, and one not usually associated with what is also a formal dining-room, is the comfortable dark green sofa. Littered with Paisley cushions, it looks as if it has been in place forever. This is one of the most coveted spots in the home.

Huge dark green bookcases run the length of two walls and, as well as books, house everything from toys and games to a refrigerator and doll's house. Designed for economy as well as for effect, the cupboard doors have been replaced with tartan fabric, ruched onto hinged rods to provide extra room for the bulky appliances stored inside.

Left: The library's striped walls and printed curtains continue the colour themes established in the drawing-room.

Below: Furniture arrangements should be adapted for different situations. As space is always in short supply when the dining-table is laid for dinner, the sofa is moved to one side of the fireplace, and a colourful ottoman joins the comfy chairs grouped around the fireplace.

Right: The billiard table, converted into a dining-table, is laid for Christmas dinner, providing a striking table setting.

Far right: By day the billiard table is home to a collection of ornaments and pot plants.

At the far end of the library is the billiard table. During the day it is covered with a sumptuous chenille cloth, but three panels, which are stored out of sight underneath the table, quickly transform it into a large dining-table. On those evenings when the dining-table is not in use, the warm glow from the wonderful red glass lamp, the books, potted plant, photographs, games and groups of decorative objects all conspire to create an essentially cosy and relaxing atmosphere.

Lighting needed to be practical and has been kept well out of harm's way. Unobtrusive wall lights, which are fixed to the bookcase, and a nineteenth-century brass lamp hanging above the billiard table contribute to this casual country-house assembly.

Nature studies and topographical and architectural pen-and-ink sketches are grouped on one wall next to a brightly coloured painting of a parrot. On the opposite wall, above the fireplace, hangs an oil painting of dogs, which has a special place in the family memories, having travelled around with us for decades. (When arranging pictures, I first position them in a pattern on the floor, then enlist some help to put them up straight!)

MASTER BEDROOM

This room is now in its second incarnation. The first was a profusion of chintz; the second cool and beige.

When economy dictates, you have to use what you have, even if it means adapting certain elements (in this instance, the corona) to suit the proportions of the room. The height of the ceiling in our previous house was three feet (one metre) lower than it is here, and in its new home the corona looked ridiculous. The problem was solved by taking the original pelmet, making it into a huge frill and attaching it to the base of the original bed curtain. This was then ruched onto an angled brass pole and fixed on the wall above the bed. The result was a delightful visual transformation, especially as the room is not only a bedroom but also a private retreat. Here is somewhere to escape to at the end of a busy day. Here I can read, or have an early night

Above: The bedroom had several striking architectural features, including a marble fireplace and a pair of tall cupboards. By adding pediments to the cupboards, their appearance was much improved, while the bookshelves make good use of an otherwise redundant space.

Above left and right: The bedroom then and now: a floral scheme of pink and blue chintz, pretty and feminine, transplanted from my previous home, and the most recent design of beige and white checks accented with black, which gives the room a stronger, more contemporary look.

with supper on a tray, watching the television. Needless to say, evenings rarely work out that way; children have a knack of crowding in post-midnight with tales of their latest conquests and escapades.

I chose the colours for the second incarnation very carefully so they wouldn't date. Whilst the currently fashionable combination of beige and white can look wonderful as an overall theme, by adding touches of black I hope I've ensured that its appeal is timeless and also given substance to the room. On a similar theme, I marbled the deep skirting-boards black at the base and painted them cream on top to detract from their overall depth.

The bed, with its sumptuous bed hangings, takes centre stage, and the walls are covered with fabric — not just for effect, but to lessen the decibels occasioned by mildly boisterous neighbours. The elaborate scroll design on the walls and the simple cotton checks work well with the black and sand fabric used for the sofa. The simple, but luxurious, dress curtains are lined, interlined, wadded along the edges

and draped over simple, unlined, checked undercurtains. This is the reverse of the bed hangings, where yards of the checked fabric are lined with beige linen.

A pair of overscaled cupboards, flanking the door, came with the apartment but looked rather like sentry boxes at Buckingham Palace. To detract from their shape and incorporate them within the structure of the room, I added quite large pediments. The simple white muslin lining on the cupboard doors softens the overall effect. Bookshelves, over the door and down either side, link the cupboards; as the shelves are only nine inches (about twenty-three centimetres) deep, extra storage space has been created behind them. At first glance, it seemed that the apartment was big enough to take care of every possession, but, as everyone knows, one is always searching for storage potential.

This is essentially a personal room. The table tops are crammed with mementoes and the desk is often piled high with the latest books, magazines and bills. The walls are lined with watercolours, portraits of the children, and pictures of the inevitable monkeys — some by renowned artists, and others, even more colourful, by the children.

Top: A desk by the bedroom window benefits from an abundance of natural light. Above right: This fabric-covered screen was specially made to conceal a radiator. It is also an elegant backdrop for the photographs and ornaments displayed on the inlaid marquetry table.

Trompe l'oeil is the most beguiling form of decorative magic

LOBBY

The lobby, which connects the library and kitchen with the upper floor, was altered to give it a more architectural appearance and to provide storage space. The ceiling was lowered and the kitchen wall cut back so that the staircase became a feature in its own right.

Four doors in such a small space would have been somewhat overbearing, so I have neatly concealed two of them behind jib doors and covered them and the walls with a colourful wallpaper that simulates bookshelves. To make the bookcases appear even more realistic, I added a paper dado rail and matching border.

The staircase walls are covered with a *trompe l'oeil* rusticated stone-effect wallpaper, which complements my *faux* library, and provides the perfect background for a series of Indian watercolours. The stairs, carpeted in dark green, lead to a half-landing, where a *trompe l'oeil* screen skilfully conceals the laundry cupboard and a small bathroom.

Above: It is hard to imagine that the trompe l'oeil screen at the top of the stairs is more than just decoration: behind it lies a laundry cupboard and bathroom.

Right: The stairway was enlivened by a rich, dark green ocelot-design carpet and an imaginative use of trompe l'oeil: faux bookshelves and stone-effect wallpaper hung with real paintings.

Left: The kitchen opens, via a small ante-room, into the conservatory. En route, you pass through a veritable gallery of blue and white china plates and their trompe l'oeil counterparts.
Below: The exterior of the conservatory and the roof terrace, a relaxing retreat from hectic city life.

Kitchen

Access to the conservatory is gained through a small, open-plan kitchen. From the beginning I thought of these two areas as wholly interdependent and absolutely made for each other. And so it has proved, both spatially and practically. The doors are painted white and decorated with a mixture of old blue and white plates and *trompe l'oeil* replicas to create a cool-looking room. The plain white walls and simple fitted cupboards and worktops contribute still further to this effect.

Conservatory and terrace

The conservatory, which leads to a large roof terrace with surprisingly spectacular views over the neighbouring gardens, was one of the main reasons I decided to embark on this unusual building conversion. It has proved a truly multi-purpose room, which acts as a laundry room and breakfast room, as well as somewhere to have impromptu lunches or sophisticated suppers.

The exterior is painted dark green, while the interior is cool, clean and white. Glass roof panels, lined with pinoleum blinds, eliminate direct sunlight and prying eyes – there is nothing worse than being the local goldfish bowl – and light oak floorboards accentuate the airy feel. An old dining-table, painted white, fits perfectly into the scheme and is surrounded by dark blue ironwork benches and chairs, which are covered with pretty cotton slip-covers.

Huge, white glass-fronted cupboards were added to house an ever-growing collection of china and glass, while the closed-in cupboards beneath are perfect for storing bulky items such as the refrigerator, washing-machine and tumble-drier out of sight.

Right and below: The conservatory is especially lovely at night, glowing with candlelight. Although intended as a family eating place, it is often used for dinner parties, the simple wooden table transformed with midnight blue, star-spangled table linen and sparkling crystal.

Lighting is the most difficult of all decorative elements in the design and decoration of a new home, and a different solution will be needed for every room. Here our problems could not have been greater as it was impossible to carry electricity into the centre of the roof. Fortunately, there was a concealed lighting track running around the edge of the conservatory to which we fixed spotlights at strategic points. Candles lend their softer light at night and a metal chandelier has added to its usefulness as a light source by becoming a highly decorative and unusual repository for coloured glass spheres.

As if by magic, the conservatory can be quickly transformed into the perfect background for entertaining: a richly coloured set of slip-covers is popped over the cushions, benches and chairs – the perfect companions for tablecloths and napkins, china, glass and arrangements of flowers, topiary or plants.

Outside, the original tarmac surface has been covered with decking, transforming the area into a beguiling roof terrace, which is more akin to an exterior room. Black iron railings – replicas of the originals – and walls covered with dark green trellis encase the area. Simple wooden

Left and below: A completely contrasting effect can be achieved with a change of colour: furnishing fabrics in checks, patterns and plains in rich plum-red tones, coordinating china and glorious over-scaled glass vases sprouting red roses complete the rich and exotic effect.

furniture and a white canvas umbrella, lined with a green and white checked fabric, are the finishing touches to a perfect setting for summer entertaining.

Nestling against the railings are groups of terracotta pots containing a variety of flowering plants such as oleander, roses, lavender and buddleia to encourage the butterflies. In the winter, a mass of clipped box, interspersed with dashes of white, emphasizes the architectural structure of the terrace. Unsightly items, such as dustbins and gardening equipment, are discreetly concealed behind unobtrusive dark green painted cupboards.

𝒫OSTSCRIPT

When I first started designing and decorating my apartment, I had two main aims: one was to create a versatile and comfortable living space for my growing family, and the other was to provide a variable space for entertaining, which would be as suitable for large, formal dinner parties as it would for more intimate family suppers. Now the work is finally completed and I must say that I am delighted with the results. For the moment I have no further plans afoot, but should another adjoining apartment become available…

CHAPTER 3

A BANKER'S RETREAT

Anyone returning home after living abroad invariably brings

back with them a substantial – and probably thoroughly

international – collection of souvenirs and objets d'art. This

certainly was the case with Nina's client, an international banker

whose career had taken him abroad for a number of years.

Far from being daunted by the eclectic nature of her

client's collection, Nina relished the opportunity of having

so many unusual objects to display, and found that work-

ing them into the decorative scheme worked like a dream.

During the years he worked abroad, Nina's client had retained a small pied à terre in London for occasional visits and recalls. On his return to England, he traded it in for a more spacious home, a couple of houses away. The decorating brief given to Nina was simple and concise: 'I would like a comfortable base that is easy on the eye, interesting to guests and well suited to a modest degree of entertaining. Above all, I need a home for my ever-expanding collection of paintings and books.'

The apartment was on two floors of a converted Edwardian house and possessed two rare and enviable features: an enormous drawing-room and a large bedroom with connecting dressing-room and bathroom. What more could a confirmed and sophisticated bachelor want or need?

Moving from a smaller to a larger home inevitably meant acquiring one or two larger and more important pieces of furniture. Once these purchases were made, however, the rest of the budget could be devoted to improvements that would transform the apartment into a highly desirable home.

> *For a house or apartment to transform convincingly into a home, it must reflect its owner's personality*

DRAWING-ROOM

When I first saw the drawing-room, my heart leapt. Although bare at the time, it had challenging proportions and superb architectural features. 'A comfortable "man's" room' was requested by my client, but he also wanted it to be a room in which a woman would feel at ease and guests completely relaxed.

The drawing-room derives its impressive size from the fact that it was originally two rooms, with a fireplace in each. When the dividing wall was removed, one fireplace was blocked in. One of the first changes I made was to build a pair of elegant, open-fronted bookcases in the recesses on either side of that blocked-in fireplace.

Although the owner's passions for paintings and books are evident throughout the apartment, they do not overshadow his other interests. Curios collected over the years, including this collection of match-strikers, are on prominent display.

Shades of sienna yellow, gold and brown, mixed with touches of red and soft green throughout the room, provide a highly suitable background for the many paintings and books. The walls are stippled yellow above the dado rail, with a *faux* Siena marble treatment below. Black skirting-boards provide a visual anchor for the room.

I decided that it was important not to let the walls look too delicate in tone; plain paint would have been too flat, whereas dragged paint would have been too grand. I therefore opted for a mildly distressed paint treatment, using a rough brush, which achieved what can only be described as a 'gentleman's club' effect.

The placing of two identical four-seater sofas, which came with the apartment, posed rather a problem. They were far too good to be sent off to an uncertain future via an auction-room, but as a pair they did nothing for the apartment. However, by covering them with different fabrics – chenille and printed linen – they look less like a pair. One is set against the back wall, between the book-cases, while the other is in front of the fireplace, with a desk behind it to make it appear much less bulky. The result is two splendidly practical and welcoming seating areas.

Left: The look my client and I had in mind for the drawing-room was masculine, yet warm and welcoming. A combination of faux marble, damask, printed linens, chenille velvet and distressed paint effects created just the richness of colour I had intended.

Above right: As well as being handsome features in their own right, the bookcases were essential to house the owner's extensive collection of books.

Rooms possessed of even modest grandeur need to have that rare quality emphasized, and here a pair of splendid Siena marble pedestals placed either side of the working fireplace achieve just that. Incidentally, they make the fireplace appear far more substantial – a welcome bonus, for it had previously seemed rather small for the room.

Two large French windows – one double, one single – give the room a wondrous natural light, which even on grey days is pleasingly suffused. Although additional lighting during the day is usually unnecessary, glamorous lighting is required after dark. Table lamps create a soft glow, while small brass floor-standing lamps are ideal for reading by.

Above: The damask curtains are dramatic and opulent, creating a delightful frame for sunlit windows on a summer's day, as well as a sumptuous and cosy retreat for cold autumn and winter nights.

If you are fortunate enough to have such spectacular, high-rising windows, flaunt them; they are potentially any room's most impressive feature. As yards of fabric were required for the elaborate swags I had in mind, I chose an inexpensive shiny damask. I then reversed it; this way, I like to think it resembles an antique fabric from a Venetian palazzo!

For the size and scale of the room, larger pieces of furniture seemed the logical choice. A grand desk in the centre of the room is the dominant feature, with its piles of books and collection of curios. A pair of gilt console tables, flanking the fireplace, add a rich touch and complement the lovely Irish black and gilt oval mirror.

Above: Ornaments, leather-bound books, catalogues and a display of orchids in a rustic container help to soften the appearance of this rather heavy and imposing desk. The warm yellow stippled walls create a neutral backdrop for an eclectic collection of paintings.

BEDROOM

The bedroom is another large and well-proportioned room. By adding bookcases and a fireplace on one wall, and a couple of small two-seater sofas – one at the foot of the bed and the other facing it – we managed to create the perfect seating area.

In this room I used darker colours: a dark teal green fabric covers the walls above the dado rail, while the walls below are painted off-white. I invariably use dark colours above and paler colours below, a treatment that prevents any room becoming overbearing and gloomy. Groups of pictures or prints on dark walls achieve a similar effect.

Above: A comfortable sofa, a collection of pictures and warm, rich colours continue the 'gentleman's club' theme established in the drawing-room, and transform the bedroom into a cosy and private retreat.

*One of the simplest and most effective ways of making a
room appear larger is to line the walls with mirror*

to open up small spaces – the room appears twice the size, and by giving the woodwork a *faux* wood treatment, the feeling of coldness effectively disappears. White floor tiles and marble tops, a white roller blind, fluffy towels and a few masculine bathroom accessories – nothing consciously accessorized – complete the transformation.

Postscript

Whether you live in a vast house or a comparatively small apartment – even one room – your main objective should be to create a home that reflects your personality by using your own possessions, whether modest or magnificent. Here, the books, prints, paintings and curios, so important to their owner, manage this most effectively, and bring the overall decorative scheme to life.

The brass wall lights with their Paisley shades are positioned on both sides of the bed and are adjustable – a 'must' for anyone with a taste for reading late at night. The rest of the room is lit with solid, brass-based table lamps.

With a few last-minute purchases – a splendid Russian roll-top desk, a desk chair with lion-headed arms, and some marvellous animal prints – the decoration was complete.

Bathroom

The bedroom connects with the dressing-room, which in turn opens into the bathroom. This was utilitarian and dull, typical of so many small bathrooms in converted houses, and was in urgent need of a complete facelift. By covering an entire wall with mirror – the best of all illusory devices

*Top: A roll-top desk means the bedroom can double-up as a study. The Victorian scrapwork screen placed in one corner diminishes the
squareness of the room. Above right: The faux wood effect on the cupboards provides a visual link with the bedroom furniture.*

CHAPTER 4

A BARONIAL CASTLE

Every designer-decorator feels a little apprehensive when preparing for a meeting with clients. This was certainly the case when Nina was approached about decorating a vast castellated Victorian-Gothic house, with additions by Clough Williams-Ellis, that notable eccentric among architects. As if to confirm her fears, Nina's meeting with the couple taking over the house verged on the melodramatic. Soon after entering her office, the husband was flat on his back with a nose-bleed, and Nina was administering ice-cubes to stem the flow.

Inevitably, the consequence of such an unfortunate event is either great embarrassment all round, or a great deal of laughter and the beginnings of a friendly relationship. Happily, the latter was the case with Nina and her clients.

The house had been a family home from its earliest days, but had become something of a burden to the owner. He therefore decided to hand over the house to his son and his family, and live in a self-contained apartment at the side of the house. Keen to move in and take on what promised to be the ideal home for themselves and their children, and the perfect gallery for their collection of modern art, Nina's clients knew only too well that the huge house needed redecorating throughout. First things first, though: they would need to establish a budget.

Such an enormous project required very detailed financial planning, organized according to priorities. Nina tackled the drawing-room, dining-room, sitting-room, study and cloakroom first; the ballroom followed a year later.

Fortunately, the house was already filled with a fine collection of furniture, which could be moved around to suit the decorative taste of the new occupants.

If you are fortunate enough to have more than one reception room,
have one gentle in style, another vibrant

Left: With two doorways, a fireplace, wide bookcase and windows taking up almost all the available wall space, the furniture had to be grouped in the centre of the room. Happily, this has created a most comfortable seating area.

Left: The vaulted ceiling created a rather oppressive, cathedral-like atmosphere, which was less than ideal in a room intended for entertaining. However, painting the beams in a broken white softened the overall effect.

DRAWING-ROOM

Rooms in Gothic-style houses tend to be of an unusual shape, and this was the case here, starting with a handsome and spacious octagonal drawing-room.

Although there were three large windows, the room was dominated by dark brown rib vaults, stretching from floor to ceiling. A grand fireplace and two sets of double doors also took their toll of the available space. A bookcase, echoing the Gothic arches of the doors, provided a token gesture towards establishing some kind of visual balance.

The most effective way of creating a light, more airy atmosphere was to paint the walls in one of my favourite background colours: palest pink – the colour of pink champagne. This colour scheme is especially successful when combined with off-white woodwork and mottled stone skirting-boards, as it is here.

Next, the curtains. Bearing in mind the room's size and the constraints of the budget, we needed something that was cost-effective in large quantities. We finally discovered just the right fabric, which was capable of hanging and draping beautifully. Echoing an expensive Italian silk, it proved ideal for a subtle, yet luxurious, treatment. Generous swags sweep up to brass rosettes fixed on a contrasting pelmet board, covered in the same fabric as the sofa. A heavy silk fringe, specially woven to match the colours of the fabric, adds a vital finishing touch.

The owners' passion for modern art is very much in evidence throughout the home. In the drawing-room, canvases by contemporary artists sit well alongside the Gothic-style architectural features. The elaborately swagged and draped taupe curtains are the perfect frame for the large French windows, which lead out into the garden.

A raspberry-coloured carpet, woven with a taupe, star-shaped design, 'holds down' the room and gives it weight. (Too pale a tone would have made the room look as if it were 'floating'.)

Then came the question of lighting and my guiding axiom: don't over-light rooms designated for entertaining. In this grand drawing-room, the lighting is discreet and ideally suited to its intended purpose. A magnificent glass chandelier in the centre of the room is controlled by a dimmer-switch, which allows for a change of mood whenever the occasion warrants. Glass table lamps with pleated shades of cream silk – white can be so glaring – illuminate the room with gentle pools of light.

Seating needed to be versatile – country houses must be flexible enough to accommodate varying numbers of guests. The large windows and limited wall space meant grouping both sofas and chairs around the fireplace and in the centre of the room.

Arranging the rest of the furniture did pose rather a problem – too many pieces would have made the room look busy, too few might have made it appear unwelcoming. The final arrangement was deemed successful by one and all. From the splendid assortment available, I chose a Queen Anne walnut bureau and a pair of gilded Gothic-style side-chairs, upholstered in pale green silk with contrasting cord and buttons.

Right: A Gothic-style chair and carved mirror-frame in one corner of the room are juxtaposed with a contemporary painting of a bandsman sitting on a park bench. With gilt detailing providing a common theme, the three look surprisingly at home with one another.
Above: Complementing the exquisite workmanship of the chair, the silk upholstery is beautifully crafted with tufted and corded detailing.

Left: Soft yellows and blues, accented with white, are a perfect foil for the elegant architectural features, including the wrought-iron picture gallery designed by Clough Williams-Ellis.

Right: My aim was to turn this wonderful, sun-filled room into an informal area where the family could relax and enjoy the views of the garden. Carpeting the floor rather than restoring the original, badly damaged flagstones was costly, but resulted in an altogether cosier atmosphere.

Above: Clough Williams-Ellis designed this suitably majestic entrance to the sitting-room, with its black and white chequered floor and Siena marble columns.

Sitting-room

The imaginative designs introduced into the sitting-room by Clough Williams-Ellis had resulted in an unusually versatile space. This well-loved room acts as the heart of the house, opening onto the staircase hall, dining-room and drawing-room. As its main function was that of family living space, where the television and stereo could be housed, it was important not to create an intimidating galleried effect.

The room now provides just the right mixture of contrasts: dramatic features, including Siena marble columns and a statue of Diana the huntress, which would not be out of place in a major art gallery, allied to an atmosphere of comfort and cosiness.

I decided to use soft yellows with blues and whites to play up the marble columns and emphasize the room's light and airy feel. After all, this is home to a young couple and their two children, so I wanted to create a fresh and, above all, welcoming scheme that was also suited to a wide range of activities. No family wants a house to look as if it has been taken straight off the designer's drawing-board and planned strictly for effect.

Even in rather grand rooms, with high ceilings,
splendid architectural features and antique furniture, a comfortable
place to relax can still be created through the
judicious use of colour and fabrics

Comfortable sofas and chairs are grouped around the fireplace, upholstered in variations on the yellow and blue theme. The tawny colours of the lattice-patterned carpet set off the paler walls above.

The curtains for the three enormous windows that overlook the garden swallowed a major portion of the budget, but we all felt they were well worth it. These are made of striped ottoman, which is a fabric that hangs particularly well, in two shades of blue and yellow. I gave shaped tops to the pelmets as I wanted to avoid having a boring line at the top of the window, and trimmed the base with a soft fringe.

In this room, lighting was of paramount importance and needed, above all, to be practical, so that any member of the family could read or write letters. The gilt wall sconces remain as part of the original decoration and I added an antique brass standard lamp. Fortunately, the room is flooded with natural light during the day, thanks to the skylight in the gallery.

Throughout the room, the furniture is displayed in what can accurately be termed a casually classical manner. After all, this is a classical room, with classical features; it is also a room where personal possessions are allowed to play their everyday roles. Piles of books, photographs, odd pieces of silver, even children's memorabilia have transformed the house into a home.

Study

The study was originally a rather pokey room, albeit with a spectacular bay window which also overlooks the rather wonderful garden. As the husband of the household needed a functional, working study, everything, bar the original elaborate gilt pelmet boards, was removed to clear the way for a simple, masculine design.

The intention was to make the room cosy and practical, a man's room. Storage and shelf space were absolutely essential. Bookcases with cupboards underneath, built along two walls, were the logical answer.

Playing up the room's ambience, I lined the walls with wallpaper the colour of manila envelopes, an excellent accompaniment for the musky-pinks, browns and bluey-greens of the curtains.

The curtain treatment is simple and well suited to the character of the room. A plain pelmet, with single pleats at either end and at the bay corners, is embellished with dark red cotton fringing, while the curtains themselves are held back with the original red and beige silk tie-backs.

A mahogany desk has been placed in the bay window to take advantage of uninterrupted views over the garden and the entrance to the house. A couple of armchairs by the fireplace are a welcome source of comfort during odd moments of reflection and relaxation, while extra seating is provided by the window seats.

Right: The Victorian pelmet boards, which were already in place when my clients moved in, formed
the starting point for the decoration of the study. Cleaned and re-gilded,
they crown a pair of floral linen curtains with dark
red cotton fringing.

DINING-ROOM

The dining-room proved an ideal place to exercise what I term 'imaginative economy'. The wall decoration, furniture and paintings were entirely appropriate, so why change them? All that was needed was a more practical arrangement that would play up, rather than detract from, the existing decoration.

Here was a large room with fine proportions and a large bay window overlooking the grounds. Rich dark green walls were embellished with a series of panels with splendid gilt mouldings – the perfect background for a collection of oil paintings. All the room needed was new curtains, carpet and a gentle wash-down.

The colour scheme I chose was dictated by the existing dark green walls. Anything too heavy or dark would only have emphasized the size of the room – dark rooms always seem to appear larger than they really are. And dining-rooms do need a touch of intimacy. We settled on golden yellow curtains with a small-scale taupe print for the chairs. A large area of exposed floorboards can look wonderful but is not always easy to live with: floorboards are apt to prove noisy and need constant attention to keep

By changing the furniture arrangement in a room, a completely different effect can be created

them well polished and in tip-top condition. Hence the choice of a taupe carpet, in this case woven with a quatre-foil pattern in various shades of green. The overall effect is sumptuous, yet cosy.

Well over one hundred yards of fabric were needed for the curtains. An inexpensive, yellow printed cotton moiré was given a wildly extravagant look with an elaborate swag pelmet, bordered with a green and golden-yellow fringe, and tie-backs. This treatment greatly enhanced the windows, which were easily grand enough to take such a colourful sweep of fabric.

Lighting is minimal – and thus glamorous. There is nothing more romantic than a candle-lit dining-room, but it is also important to be able to see your food. A pair of elaborate gilt sconces and a huge glass chandelier provide soft overall lighting, sufficient for dining by and suitable for intimate conversation.

Most of the furniture was already in place and needed little more than repositioning and tender loving care to make the room appear more inviting and more aesthetically pleasing. The bay, however, looked very empty and stark, and clearly needed attention. Imagine the joy when we discovered two large candelabra in another part of the house. Standing on hand-painted plinths emulating stone, they look terrific.

Left: The bay windows, giving a panoramic view of the castle grounds, called for a dramatic treatment of handsomely swagged and draped golden-yellow printed cotton moiré.
Right: Dark green and gold are a traditional dining-room colour partnership in English country houses. No other combination would set off the glass and silverware so successfully and enhance the natural beauty of the mahogany table and rosewood sideboard.

ℬALLROOM

My brief for the magnificent circular ballroom was simple but comprehensive. The room needed to be sufficiently flexible to be used as a ballroom for parties and dances; as a tea room; as an ante-room to a lecture hall and, even more important, as an art gallery. My clients' ever-changing (perhaps, more accurately, ever-growing) art collection needed display space.

Any designer-decorator welcomes a challenge that demands starting from scratch. I decided to be fearless and give the room an exotic and unexpected rebirth. The problem here was clear. The ballroom had the potential to be quite spectacular but was, at present, a dead space – there was no furniture, acres of floorboards and three enormous windows. A cheerful, wide-striped, Regency-style wallpaper was my first step. Far too often we are told that

Above: Regency-style stripes, a contemporary painting of a dancing couple and an arched Gothic-style doorway illustrate the ballroom's successful blend of historic and modern-day decorating styles.

paintings must be hung against a pale grey background. My approach couldn't have been more different – but somehow it works. Even small pictures hung in groups look impressive against strong backgrounds.

The overall effect is drama with colour as the keynote. When starting to decorate large, empty rooms, particularly in Britain, always take the weather into consideration. Such rooms can look marvellous on bright sunny days but dauntingly grim on grey days, especially with grand windows like these. Bold red and white walls and charming off-white curtains, bordered with raspberry ribbon, provided the answer. The combination evokes a real sense of warmth, helped by the colours of the adjacent billiard-room and by the modern paintings.

The design for the curtains was taken from an old decoration primer that I have. By using the original pelmet boards and yards of inexpensive ribbon, it was possible to make the curtains without considerable outlay on other expensive decorative touches.

But the main consideration is, of course, the paintings. When was anyone last in a ballroom that doubled as an art gallery and with such enormous panache?

Cloakroom

The stark, black and white marbled hall leads directly to a cloakroom. Featuring two white-painted 'his-and-hers' cubicles, it is a wonderfully light room with huge windows overlooking the gardens.

The cloakroom did not need a great deal of money spent on it because everything was in such good shape. I wasn't at all bothered by the exposed pipework; burying it in the walls would have been an unbelievable waste of money – and for what?

Originally, the upper areas of the walls were painted a dull green, which gave the room a chilly, 'municipal-utility' look. Yet the room also had shoulder-high, white wall tiles with black borders, black and white marble floor tiles and chic black marble-clad basins – resplendent with original fittings. What more is needed?

Bright and airy, with chic black marble-clad basins and a black and white chequered floor already in place, the cloakroom needed only the embellishments of a full-length mirror and a few plants.

Black and white with terracotta paintwork is a splendid combination, especially if you jolly it up with plants and a mirror. In this instance, a splendid mahogany and gilt-framed dressing-mirror proved the perfect solution. I was also delighted to be able to demonstrate that very often a simple room needs only one over-scaled piece to prevent it from becoming dull.

Postscript

I was as delighted with this commission as my clients were with the final result. We were all very much aware that, with such an ambitious venture, it was absolutely essential to establish a budget at the very beginning of the project, so that both parties would know exactly where they stood at any one moment.

Working closely together, we succeeded in achieving our principal goals: the sitting-room is very much the heart of the home, and the beautiful ballroom is now ready to be used to its full potential.

CHAPTER 5

NEW FOR OLD

A year after decorating their London pied à terre, Nina was asked by her South African clients to find another, larger property for them. The reason? They had fallen in love with the city and wanted to spend more time there.

The four-bedroomed house that Nina acquired proved ideal: light and airy, with spacious rooms for entertaining. It was decided, though, at the outset, to convert the four bedrooms into one master bedroom, complete with two en suite dressing-rooms and bathrooms, and a guest-room.

There was one important stipulation in Nina's brief: all the furniture from the previous apartment had to be used in the new home. 'But why not?' reasoned Nina.

Using a similar colour scheme to that of the apartment, and with her customary flair, she incorporated every piece of furniture. The mix of old and new was quite a coup, especially as the new setting was so different, and, as it turned out, more suited to her clients' possessions. Fortunately, the basics from the apartment, such as the soft furnishings, rugs and dining-room furniture, were perfectly appropriate for re-use here, and so Nina was able to use the new budget to purchase a few coveted antique pieces and other decorative 'musts'.

*Wide floorboards in a small,
narrow room will make the room appear
more spacious*

ENTRANCE HALL

To evoke a sense of space in the small and narrow entrance hall, I laid wide floorboards – narrow planks would have accentuated the narrowness of the passage, making it appear longer than it really is. (If you really have no alternative but to use narrow floorboards, you could try laying them in a herring-bone pattern. As well as being far more pleasing to the eye, this also succeeds in reducing the elongating effect.)

Cream damask wallpaper and a beige stair carpet also helped in creating the desired feeling of space, but meant that an injection of colour was definitely called for. Hence the choice of bright yellow taffeta curtains – an eighteenth-century design with baskets of doves and pink roses, held back with brass embrasures – which look positively translucent when the sun filters through.

Recessed spotlights illuminate the entrance hall with soft pools of light. (Table lights were a tempting alternative here, but it was agreed they would take up too much space and might get knocked over.)

An unusual hat-stand, facing the front door, is a practical as well as decorative addition, displaying an eclectic collection of hats – from shooting hats to straw hats – and creates a casual and informal atmosphere.

INNER HALL

Imposing double doors lead into the spacious inner hall. Although its main role is that of a reception room, by introducing a small dining-table and chairs my clients are able to use it as an informal dining-area, too. With the addition of the simple stone fireplace, the room feels more inviting.

Relocating the furniture from the apartment to the house was an immensely exciting, and rewarding, aesthetic challenge for me. The eighteenth-century console table, the gold, white and grey painted mirror with the American eagle on top, and the octagonal dining-table and chairs were originally in the drawing-room of my clients' apartment, but here, in the inner hall of their new house, they have taken on a new lease of life and look completely different.

By using identical curtains, flooring and off-white walls, I succeeded in creating a harmonious link between the inner hall and the entrance hall. Introducing subtle shades of grey plays up the existing colours – incidentally, the bright yellow painting hanging above the console table was the key to my choice of colour scheme. It was essential that colour and scale were well balanced. On the mantelpiece, small china tubs filled with yellow and purple pansies make a pretty contribution to this sense of calm equilibrium.

*Left: Small entrance halls are notoriously difficult to light. With no room for bulky table lamps,
small, unobtrusive, recessed ceiling lights proved a practical solution.
Above: Rather than lay carpets or heavy rugs throughout the inner and entrance halls, I decided to leave the floorboards
bare to create a light, summery feel.*

Drawing-room

The L-shaped drawing-room had one major drawback: no fireplace, which was really quite unusual in this style of house. Somehow the omission meant that it was difficult to create an inviting seating area, but that was speedily rectified by the purchase and installation of a lovely French, white marble chimney-piece, deep enough to accommodate a grate, although there was no flue.

Originally comprising two rooms, the drawing-room had since been opened up to create one large room. The space allows for two seating areas: a larger and more formal arrangement which is grouped around the fireplace at the front of the house, and, to the rear, a less formal study-cum-library, with cupboards housing television, stereo and other forms of home entertainment.

The colour scheme was dictated by the need to re-use the furnishings: a pair of sofas upholstered in a yellow and grey-green floral linen; two rugs designed to partner the

Reflections in mirror glass, lining the wall space between windows, create a sense of mystery

sofas; and two armchairs covered in blue chenille. To create a complementary, yet different, overall effect, we lined the walls with a vibrant yellow, self-patterned fabric – an excellent background colour for paintings and mirrors, and one too often neglected by faint-hearted decorators, professional and amateur alike. A pair of French chairs, upholstered in a dark green Fortuny fabric, and needlework cushions provide vibrant splashes of colour, without being too intrusive.

The curtains proved to be the colour keynote for the drawing-room. In order to bring together all the colours in the room, including the dark green of the chairs, and to

As the house is fairly small, it was important to introduce a sense of continuity into the colour scheme. The drawing-room picks up the themes established in the inner hall – sunny yellows, soft greys and blues – but the chairs and striped silk taffeta curtains introduce a new colour note of pale grey-green.

The drawing-room has been adapted for both recreation and work. The chairs and sofa surrounding the coffee table create a natural area for relaxation, while at the opposite end of the room is a study area complete with writing desk and pedimented bookcase – also home to the television and stereo.

make a change from the plain curtains in the previous apartment, I had a silk taffeta woven in green, blue, yellow and cream. Light in texture and lively in pattern, it immediately lifts the room, giving an impression of gaiety, and creates a welcoming atmosphere.

The three windows at the front of the drawing-room have ceiling-high pelmets to give height. I like generously proportioned pelmets: two inches (five centimetres) of pelmet per foot (per thirty centimetres) of curtain length is my rule of thumb. Deep pelmets give a room a wonderful sense of grandeur, whereas ungenerous pelmets create the opposite effect.

Mirror, lining the walls between the windows, is hung with pictures and smaller gilt-framed mirrors. This effectively breaks up the dominance of three sets of curtains, creating a touch of glamour and an air of mystery. Some guests even confess to a mild difficulty in working out where the room begins and ends, an impression emphasized by the exceptionally generous natural light that floods the room from both ends.

For artificial lighting, I used gilt candle sconces with little French candle bulbs and placed them either side of the fireplace; an angled lamp for reading; a pair of hurricane lamps on the chimney-piece and handsome porcelain lamps for table and desk. The overall effect is usually subdued, thanks to dimmer switches, yet it can be brighter when the occasion requires.

Seating grouped around the fireplace provides an elegant, yet comfortable and surprisingly flexible, area for relaxation. A large sofa faces the fireplace, with two deep chairs on one side and a pair of pretty French chairs on the other. A large coffee table in the centre and a long stool in front of the fire make gossip, and even serious discussion, irresistible in this setting. Eight or ten can sit here comfortably, and a few easy-to-manoeuvre lightweight chairs dotted around the room can always be included should the size of the party grow.

Pictures were re-framed to blend with the decorative scheme. Although so far from home, these South African paintings look just right in their new surroundings.

Above and below: Don't be afraid to use a bold pattern lavishly. In the master bedroom the same glorious rose print
features on walls, curtains and eiderdown. Broken up at intervals by the pink and cream of the bed drapery and the breakfront cupboard
— actually a cupboard and doors to the two en suite dressing rooms — the pattern never becomes overwhelming.

MASTER BEDROOM SUITE

The master bedroom suite takes up the whole of one floor of the house. Originally consisting of two bedrooms and one bathroom, the floor was converted to create one bedroom with his-and-hers en suite dressing-rooms and bathrooms.

Taking immediate advantage of the extra space that this conversion released, I was able to incorporate a small lobby, for every square inch of space is valuable, both visually and physically.

Undoubtedly my greatest challenge was how to disguise the number of randomly placed doors in the master bedroom. By positioning a specially designed cupboard in between the two dressing-room doors, we succeeded in creating what looked like a breakfront cupboard — an elegant as well as a practical disguise.

I used a beautiful rose-patterned material for the walls, curtains and eiderdown. To prevent the abundance of pattern overpowering the room, the half-tester, headboard and bed valance are in a cream fabric, while the lining for the half-tester is an enchanting pink and white striped silk.

Generously gathered pelmets have shaped bases trimmed with deep rose-pink fan edging, while the curtains themselves, swept up into fabric tie-backs, tumble gently onto the carpet. Mirror is again used between the windows, this time detracting from a take-over bid by yards of rose-patterned chintz!

Lighting is appropriately subdued, yet perfect for reading by. I placed the bedside lights inside the curtains because, despite the size of the room, there was insufficient space for large bedside tables on which to place lamps.

Cloakroom

When decorating really small rooms, my simple, albeit rather dramatic, advice is: Go over the top! Do your own thing and practise your secretly held desires. In this cloakroom, the theory is well demonstrated, with the walls and ceiling completely covered with a large-patterned fabric. The result is a visual knock-out.

Surprisingly, a tiny room is often the best place to indulge in dramatic, overscaled designs. A few carefully chosen accessories help to establish a sense of scale in this cloakroom.

I moved the basin from its original location behind the door to create more space, and replaced the recessed lighting with a splendid Indian bell lantern, positioning it centrally within the ornate tented ceiling.

Postscript

Decorating my clients' new home was a question of creating a completely different look from that of their old apartment, while using the same pieces of furniture and decorative possessions. (Fortunately, the budget did allow me to introduce some antique furniture and accessories for certain parts of the house.)

The end result delighted us all. We managed to rehouse everything and my clients seemed ready to settle down in their idyllic new home. Imagine, then, when seemingly so cosily ensconced, they casually remarked, 'If you happen to hear of a slightly larger house in the right area, Nina, do let us know...'

This certainly came as rather a shock. I recovered, however, to await events. After all, I realized long ago that, for some, home-making can be as much of a hobby as ocean-cruising in luxury liners can be to others. Yet, I have to admit that, in my profession, I cannot think of anything more rewarding than to be asked by clients on three occasions to decorate their new homes.

A beautifully decorated study is a great inducement to settling down to work. The addition of a few of the owner's best-loved pictures makes this a room where he can instantly feel at ease.

$\mathcal{E}$AST MEETS WEST

When a businessman from Hong Kong bought a 1930s neo-Georgian house in the south of England, it was Nina he approached to transform his newly acquired home into the quintessential English country house.

The sheer size and scope of the commission necessitated a meeting with her client in London, followed by a trip to Hong Kong, before Nina's blueprint was finalized. At the planning stage, she worked closely with the architect, after which she was responsible for decorating the entire house.

This included the buying of period furniture and decorative objects. Indeed, virtually everything in the house, except the paintings for the reception rooms, was her responsibility.

Nina's brief included the conversion of several reception rooms, fourteen bedrooms and five bathrooms into eight bedrooms with en suite bathrooms and dressing rooms. Nevertheless, the most time-consuming and expensive part of the project was repairing the windows, of which there were over a hundred!

From start to finish, this challenging commission took just under a year. Nina's intention at the outset was to create a home that looked as if a family had been in residence for at least forty years. This she achieved with enormous success, not only through her choice of fabrics and furniture but also by building up an extensive library of magazines and books. Indeed, she bought virtually everything a family could possibly need, right down to the coat hangers, the soap, even the sunhats.

Hall

A long, wide corridor links the small entrance lobby to what is now the main hall. I realized that if I were to create an authentic country-house feeling in this complex of corridors, lobbies and halls, I was going to need lots of old runners and rugs to lend warmth and colour.

Bearing in mind the enormous area that needed to be covered, antique rugs were certainly out of the question. My only alternative was to find a carpet with a border that could be cut and joined together to resemble a rug. Fortunately, a trip to Paris unearthed the solution: a delightful old-fashioned design of deep blue, soft green and straw yellow against a rust background. It was, indeed, one of those rare carpets that can be trusted to underpin the entrance to almost any country house.

Throughout the hall, colours are linked without looking as if they have been professionally 'matched'. Maize yellow walls and straw yellow curtains – yellow has that wonderful ability to mix with most colours – work well with the striped chair fabric, which looks extremely expensive but was, in fact, very reasonably priced.

The unusual round-headed windows were awkward to dress. Rather than conceal their shape, I decided to emphasize it, using curtains with pinch pleats which follow the arch of each window.

Lighting was something of a nightmare. I decided against small, recessed spotlights because, quite frankly, they're not 'English country house'. In any case, I had the good fortune to find a set of nine Anglo-Indian glass lanterns. These, together with soft lighting in the alcoves and the odd table lamp, cast an altogether balanced light.

Instead of trying to disguise the rather awkward shape of the windows in the hall, I chose to emphasize them

Drawing-room

The drawing-room was a dream of a room: a magnificent rectangular space with a run of four windows and a French door leading onto the gardens. At one end of the room there was a wonderfully grand, eighteenth-century white marble fireplace with black reeded columns. The ceilings were embellished with unusual mouldings.

My job was to transform this enormous space into a formal drawing-room, complete with two seating areas, side tables and a grand piano. However, first things first: grand rooms need grand planning. It was all extremely challenging and, let's face it, rather frightening.

What, I asked myself, could be more impressive than cream silk damask for the walls and curtains? These, teamed with the striped silk taffeta undercurtains and cushions, rare Aubusson carpets and fine tapestry on the ottoman, simply have to be the grandest combination imaginable.

Such a dignified plan required a sophisticated curtain treatment, hence my choice of elaborate swags and tails with billowing silk undercurtains which are drawn at night to prevent a feeling of claustrophobia. Narrow mirrors fitted between the windows add a touch of nocturnal glamour and sparkle to the room.

Rough matting on the floor prevents what could have been a rather grand 'Versailles' look from taking over the drawing-room completely. Besides, such matting is an excellent neutral background for any rug or carpet, however sumptuous, and allows them to stand out without competing for attention. Incidentally, the carpets I chose aren't a pair, but their similar colours and dimensions ensure that they work extremely well together.

Left: Large country halls can be intimidating spaces, but this one has a decidedly informal atmosphere, thanks to its decoration. The circular table, decorated with flowers and books, provides a stylish focal point in what could have seemed a never-ending expanse of walls and windows.

A large drawing-room needs plenty of seating, and by choosing different types of chair and sofa, we managed to create a feeling of intimacy and comfort. To either side of the fireplace I placed a slipper chair – a useful extra to any conversation area – and a three-seater sofa, with a slightly rounded back, and a *bergère*.

The far end of the room had no fireplace, and needed a rather impressive piece as a focal point. The answer: a lovely, walnut, Queen Anne bureau bookcase, with three finials which had the advantage of giving extra height. A corner banquette, deep and comfortable and able to accommodate six to eight people, provides additional seating.

The lighting comprises mainly table lamps and a pair of Venetian twisted glass standing lamps. (Whenever I saw a lamp base that I liked on my shopping expeditions for the

house, I bought it. I then moved and changed bases around as I decorated the various rooms.) The beautiful etched and gilded glass column lamps on side tables flanking the fireplace are antique. I think lampshades should always be hand-picked. Their shapes go in and out of fashion, not that that matters unduly, but a change of lampshade is an excellent way of updating a room. Here, we used a wide variety of fabrics and shapes.

Undoubtedly, my client will add paintings as he finds them. A house that is complete from the minute the owner walks in is not an ideal home. In the early stages a room needs to be 'en route', as it were. You should be able to invite your friends to a party without being embarrassed that it's 'not quite finished'. Paintings and objects can, and will, follow, as will other adornments.

Left: Juxtaposing cushions of different designs on a sofa adds a colourful finishing touch to the decoration of the drawing-room. A boldly striped silk taffeta cushion in raspberry, cream and green sits alongside a green and cream crown and leaf design, embellished with two corner rosettes and tasselled cords. Above: Cream silk damask walls and curtains provide a cool background for the rich hues of the cushions. Above right: Large, airy and well proportioned, the drawing-room was a joy to decorate. The two Aubusson carpets set the tone for the room's decoration: a medley of reds, soft yellows and greens.

BILLIARD ROOM

If you are lucky enough to have the space, a billiard room is a joyous escape for the men in the party — especially in large houses destined for entertaining a large number of people.

The billiard room has three large windows, which are somewhat shaded by the overhanging colonnade. But no matter. This is, after all, a games room, and should be treated as such with appropriate seating, and, of course, discreet cupboards housing drinks, glasses and the telephone. My main objective was to make the room comfortable and inviting, but still obviously a masculine domain.

To highlight the masculine feel, I based the colours on a splendid shade of plum, and, as if donated by a patron saint of decorators, a marvellous rug with a plum background and lots of green, blue and yellow tones appeared as if by magic. This has proved tough, thick and deep enough to withstand the heavy billiard table.

Rich aubergine damask wallpaper and olive green, aubergine and caramel striped curtains — their simplicity emphasized with plain mahogany poles and finials — enforce the room's sobriety still further. Another lucky 'find' was a pair of billiard benches which were re-upholstered in sumptuous velvet, echoing the overall colour scheme.

Whilst accessorizing the billiard room, I made what I was told was a forgivable blunder. My client had a beautiful painting of a plum tree, embellished with Chinese calligraphy. I despaired of finding a wall high enough on which to hang this newly acquired treasure. In desperation I telephoned Hong Kong, only to learn that I had been trying to hang the painting the wrong way up: vertically rather than horizontally!

STUDY

One of my client's few formal requests was an oak-panelled study; I wasn't at all surprised. I often think panelled studies are what every foreigner dreams of having as their personal retreat in an archetypal English country house!

Small, with high ceilings and somewhat unbalanced proportions, the study was obviously going to be rather a challenge. Traditional bookcases with elegant pediments, placed either side of the fireplace, were the perfect formula for giving the room its feeling of intimacy and seclusion. (Bookcases to the ceiling would have been daunting, accentuating the high ceiling.) Although the bookcases are well lit from inside, a pair of shelf-based porcelain lamps with off-white shades help to make the room appear cosier.

A well-proven decorator's trick for giving the impression of a lower ceiling, and one that works particularly well in smaller rooms, is to create a mottled effect on the ceiling. Here, I've used cream paint to give just a hint of colour.

The study carpet is a rich taupe with a red Gothic star motif. As the rooms on this floor of the house all lead off the hall, with its wide area of floorboards that acts as a breathing space, we could afford to lay different carpets in each room. (A mix of different coloured carpets in an area where rooms lead from one to another can prove rather disturbing to the eye; a sense of unity is essential for such a setting.)

Bright red and other warm colours enliven the oak panelling while the heavy wool curtains with gathered pelmets to the ceiling allow the maximum amount of light into the room. A sofa, a pair of comfortable armchairs and a partner's desk complete the transformation of the study.

Above left and above: Both the study and the neighbouring billiard room are markedly masculine in style, with colour schemes based on rich tones of dark red. The aubergine damask wallpaper in the billiard room is balanced by off-white paintwork below the dado rail which prevents a sombre atmosphere. Shades of tomato red in the study are perfect foils for the grey marbled fireplace and oak panelling.

*A hand-painted mural is a unique and original
alternative to paintings when there is a huge
expanse of wall to cover*

DINING-ROOM

The original dining-room had a conventional oblong dining-table, which was capable of seating eighteen people. However, we needed to observe the Chinese custom of eating at a circular table, with a 'lazy Susan' (or revolving tray) in the centre. Accordingly, I commissioned a round table from David Linley. This beautiful piece seats eight, but will take twelve when the extensions are added. As a back-up for larger dinner parties, a collapsible hardboard table, which also seats eight, is brought in, creating seating for a grand total of twenty. When both tables are in use, they are covered with short cream damask cloths over floor-length red cloths, so that they look like a pair.

In order to make this room feel less rectangular, I commissioned a mural for three sides of the room, depicting an eighteenth-century golfing scene, which effectively combines my client's passion for golf and the painting style of Claude Lorrain. The fourth wall is made up of the windows, but the mirror on the small area of wall between the windows reflects the mural on the opposite side of the room. The Venetian candle lights, fixed to the mirror, give a wonderful twinkle of light at night.

The splendid, English, eighteenth-century mantelpiece made of white marble was already in place and now stands out beautifully against the mural. A pair of unusual wine coolers look thoroughly at home in their setting either side of the chimney-piece.

The floor was another challenge. We didn't want to cover the beautiful floorboards entirely with wall-to-wall carpet, but we did need something that would work regardless of whether one or two dining-tables were in use. The

solution was a trip to Paris and a specially commissioned rug, made to our choice of colours – a deep blue background with the pattern in reds, soft greens and sand.

By this point, there was so much going on in the room that I needed a curtain fabric that would blend into the background rather than dominate, hence curtains of soft green silk with heavy cord tassel tie-backs.

The comfortable dining-chairs, which are covered in a French fabric depicting trees and leaves, are copies of eighteenth-century originals.

Good, overall lighting was requested for the dining-room: a pair of modern, glass, urn-shaped bases with sea green shades and two mahogany standing lamps, which can be moved around to create a more general light, meet the brief.

Far left: Mirror, lining the wall from ceiling to dado rail, with Venetian candle lights attached, creates magical lighting effects at night.
Above left and above: A blend of European and Oriental styles, the dining-room features a colourful golfing mural and two circular tables: one an exquisite hand-made piece by David Linley, the other, concealed beneath a red cloth, an inexpensive hardboard version.

Large-patterned fabrics and wallpapers are best suited to large rooms where they will not overwhelm

MASTER BEDROOM SUITE

The master bedroom suite is enormous, occupying one entire side of the house. Here, I have used a cream linen fabric on the walls and soft blue carpet throughout, allowing the rooms to integrate with each other.

A spacious room is ideal for using large amounts of pattern because there is no chance that the room will appear swamped. So, deliberately avoiding anything that would give the room an obviously feminine look, we chose a charming linen print in shades of soft rosy pink, blue-green and

taupe with an off-white background for the window curtains, bed drapery and day-bed.

Such generous amounts of pattern and colour need skilful accessorizing or they can end up looking monotonous. To prevent this from happening and also to establish an important link, I added heavy fringing to the bed and curtain pelmets, while lining the bed hangings in cream. The cream cotton piqué bedspread is bound in blue, and the stool at the end of the bed covered in tapestry brings additional colour, texture and pattern.

Lights within the four-poster bed allow for reading in bed without having to fumble for light switches outside the curtain. Fitted to the wall behind, the lamps just pop through a slit made in the lining.

Little wonder the bedroom is so comfortable with an armchair and day-bed in front of the fireplace. Botanical prints line the walls and a handsome black and gilt mirror hangs above the fireplace.

Left: Bold floral patterns can be given free rein in larger rooms, as there is little risk of them dominating their surroundings.

Above right: A fireplace is always a luxury in a bedroom, and luckily this white marble Regency chimney-piece was already in place. Its classic design ensures that it doesn't look intrusive against the gentle colour scheme of soft blues and rose pinks.

Beyond the sitting-room and dressing-room, the walls of which are lined with mahogany cupboards, is the spacious bathroom. Despite its size, this was a difficult room to plan, as the fireplace and windows took up most of the wall space. Fitting the bath between the windows was both a practical and luxurious solution: it is possible to lie back in the bath and gaze out to the garden. Complete with a walk-in shower and two basins, this is an extremely covetable bathroom.

Guest bedroom suite

A thorough architectural overhaul transformed what was a rabbit warren of passages and cubby holes into a twin bedroom complete with a cosy seating area, dressing-room and enormous bathroom.

Above: A centrally placed bath allows the bather a splendid view of the garden. Below: An all-over treatment of blue and white toile de Jouy made the awkward proportions of the bedroom less obvious.

At the far end of the room, built-in cupboards resemble a bookcase, their plain glass panels lined with fabric to prevent any hint of heaviness. To one side an oval dressing-table, covered with a smaller patterned, blue and white floral fabric, adds to the many charms of the room.

Two round, frosted ceiling lights, a desk lamp, a pair of dressing-table lamps with rather eccentric shades, lamps to either side of the fireplace and bedside lights for reading by ensure flexible lighting.

The blue and white theme extends into the guest bathroom where it includes touches of brown, with brown, blue and white curtain fabric and periwinkle blue dragged walls, a colourful context for the pair of white pedestal basins and Victorian bath, placed lengthways in front of the window.

℘OSTSCRIPT

This long-term commission has proved to be one of the most rewarding. I knew I had fulfilled my brief to transform the house into 'a comfortable home where English friends will feel at ease' when my client first set foot in his new home and exclaimed, 'My dream has come true.'

This is a favourite room – a tribute to the Orient's love of blue and white. Blue and white fabric is everywhere, save on the sofa and bed covers. Initially I considered using this design in the main bedroom but it works more successfully here as it detracts from the dimensions of this long, awkward room.

The walls, covered with a blue and white toile de Jouy fabric depicting pagodas, are edged with plain blue braid. I particularly wanted the wall and curtain fabric to be the same so that guests would not have to lie in bed facing acres of mismatching fabric. As the windows were rather wide for their height, I used a Gothic-shaped pelmet to break up the length. It also complements the pagoda shapes.

This large room could easily look empty and uninviting, but a sofa and two four-foot (1.2-metre) single beds instead of two of standard size guarantee comfort. The cotton piqué bed covers provide a cool, clean contrast; and plump eiderdowns add that ultimate luxurious touch.

Top: Sadly, dressing-tables are apt to be overlooked these days, despite their luxurious appearance when accessorized with silver-backed brushes and a mirror: in this case, a triple mirror with a blue glass surround. Above right: In the guest bathroom, every comfort has been considered, with a chaise longue positioned in front of the fire. The bath is sited next to the window, but cream blinds ensure privacy during the day.

$\mathcal{S}$MALL BUT STYLISH

Nina recalls, somewhat wryly, the rather inauspicious

beginnings to this decorating commission. She was asked to

transform what had once been a family apartment into a

comfortable and stylish home for two. The small, London

pied à terre had been lived in for many years by the

younger generation. The scene of many wild parties, it had

been treated with carefree abandon and needed a complete

overhaul. An additional challenge confronting Nina was

the unusual shape of the building – it was completely round.

To make matters even worse, all the rooms were narrow, and there were no redeeming architectural features to speak of, only awkward beams, narrow doorways and long corridors: all in all, a typical 1930s building.

Nina's decorating brief was both comprehensive and concise: 'Make the place attractive and easy to run. After all, this is an eighth-floor apartment and the light positively streams in through the windows. Doesn't that mean you're half-way there? Isn't natural light an apartment's best feature?'

Books are an overlooked but reliable way of introducing colour into a room

DRAWING-ROOM/DINING-ROOM

My initial reaction after visiting the apartment for the first time was that this long, narrow room would work far more successfully if it were divided into two separate areas – one for sitting, the other for dining.

If such a division is planned, it is wise to make the divisive element something special, both practically and visually. In this case, I decided to design an unusually deep set of bookshelves. Measuring fifteen inches (thirty-eight centimetres) deep, the shelves, which reach all the way to the ceiling, incorporate low cupboards to create much needed extra storage space. 'Pierced' to allow for movement between the two new rooms, the shelves flank a handsome, reeded, rectangular arch, which performs its linking task extremely well: a sound foundation for the scheme.

The bookshelves underwrite the success of this two-room enterprise, creating a cosy atmosphere with their colourful contents (books can always be relied upon to bring colour to a room). By lining the backs of the shelves with marbled paper, I was able to introduce even more colour.

Another excellent source of colour in this room derives from the cushions, which also add texture and pattern – a mixture that enhances the overall effect of any room.

On entering what is now the sitting/dining area for the first time, I was confronted by an incredibly long, corridor-like space. My first step – installing ceiling-high bookshelves – created two much more elegantly proportioned rooms. The deep shade of red used in the dining-room, glimpsed through the rectangular reeded arch, also helps to shorten the room by 'bringing in' the far wall.

When I first took on this decorating project, there were only four huge armchairs and three rather ugly tables in the room – that was all. The most practical seating arrangement was to place a pair of sofas either side of the fireplace and a stool in front of the fire. This arrangement created a sizeable conversation area, and it is one that has proved extremely successful as the small apartment is frequently used for entertaining.

Fortunately, there was just enough space between the windows to accommodate a drop-front writing desk. A splendid antique wing chair, positioned in front of the bookshelves and backed by the window, provides a well-lit retreat for reading. At night, a brass arm-light between the desk and chair provides additional light for writing or reading by, while wall lights to either side of the fireplace and table lamps at either end of the sofas, as well as on the drinks table, create a good overall light.

If the shape of the room allows, a round table is the best choice for a small dining area, and more convivial

To introduce a touch of grandeur, I covered the walls with a light taupe, self-stripe wallpaper – vertical stripes are a very simple way of making ceilings appear higher. I then used a charming red, blue and stone fabric for the curtains and a stone linen for the sofas which then blended in with the walls – bright or dark colours stand out, emphasizing bulky shapes. Last, but not least, the wing chair is covered in a mole grey chenille velvet, which echoes the colour scheme of the room.

The curtain treatment, on the other hand, is simple – elaborate curtains would only have drawn attention to the awkward proportions of the room. My intention was to create an impression of height using French curtain headings on self-covered tracks; pelmets would have been far too fussy and overwhelming and would have encroached into the room space.

The unusual shape of the building was sharply revealed to me when the carpet-layer asked how I wanted the carpets seamed. It was only then that I realized how circular the rooms actually were. To detract from this effect, I chose a plain taupe carpet – an old favourite of mine – and used it throughout the reception rooms, which also succeeds in making the apartment appear larger than it really is.

The adjoining dining-room has red lacquered walls which, when viewed from the drawing-room, give a welcoming impression of warmth and depth. Inside, there is just enough space to house the essentials: a round table (which, luckily, fitted into the available space), half-a-dozen chairs and a sideboard.

Above: A symmetrical arrangement of sofas, tables and lamps on opposite sides of the room gives the drawing-room an elegance that belies its narrow proportions. Right: Carrying the wonderful deep raspberry red of the drawing-room chintz through to the walls, lampshades and flowers of the dining-room establishes a sense of continuity.

Bedroom suite

In the bedroom my problems were magnified – and curiously reversed. As my clients wanted this small space to house a double bed and rows of cupboards, I decided to convert what were originally two small rooms into one, not-so-small room. Although the end result was *still* a small room, it was a far more effective use of the limited space. To cap it all, though, the back wall was shorter than the curved front wall, adding to my problems!

I approached the basic alterations rather as if I had been commissioned to glorify an Edwardian royal railway carriage, installing cupboards at one end of the room, with additional cupboards and a dressing-table at the other. We even managed to make room for a tiny, en suite dressing-room and bathroom.

Very often the only way to tackle small rooms is to cover them from top to bottom in fabric. In this instance, I used a spectacular blue and white fabric for the walls, curtains, and upholstery – a solid colour would have made the bedroom look more like a cell. This immediately gave the room interest, which was certainly not a quality it possessed at the start of the proceedings.

The low ceilings determined the style of the curtains. Once again, it was important to keep them neat and unfussy, using a treatment that gave an impression of height: simple, French-headed curtains on covered tracks were the answer.

The walls behind the bed are lined with attractive black and white prints of family portraits, which were left over from a previous house. As they are monochrome, they do not compete with the flamboyant fabric on the walls. The opposite wall is decorated with a rather eccentric mirror and some simple flower prints.

The end result is a surprisingly comfortable room with plenty of storage space, provided by the white fitted cupboards running the length of one wall.

Leading off the bedroom is a long 'slip' of a bathroom, lined in white tile, with the occasional blue floral tile let in to soften the effect. The mirrors, which are framed in blue to inject a little more colour, create a feeling of space.

Postscript

In this apartment I needed to create space without compromising on the practicalities. By transforming two tiny bedrooms into one, and one long reception room into a dining-room and drawing-room, I was able to create a far more comfortable arrangement.

*Above: The bathroom, another
long, narrow room, called
for a minimalist approach,
with white fittings, wall tiles
and marble splashback (backsplash). The mirrors succeed
in making the room appear
larger than it really is.
Left: This small bedroom,
devoid of architectural detail,
desperately needed visual
interest. This was supplied by
the fresh blue and white tree of
life design used for the curtains,
walls and upholstery. A
scalloped-edged bedspread,
matching the bedside table edge,
is a pretty decorative touch.*

As a frequent visitor to the apartment, I know that this new decorating scheme works. The apartment has become a practical, yet comfortable, space where everything looks made for its purpose. Living in a small space is a problem only if you are not well organized. You need to be a little ruthless and, from time to time, go through your personal possessions to decide what are the absolute essentials to retain and then get rid of anything that is at all superfluous.

Our next step will be to deck out the terrace. This will create an exterior room, somewhere to dine or sit during the warm summer months. Little by little we are adding the finishing touches...

CHAPTER 8

AN ENGLISH COUNTRY HOUSE

Once Nina's clients had overcome their excitement at becoming

the owners of a handsome William and Mary country house,

they began to discuss the issue of its decoration, and

contacted the one designer-decorator they both had in mind.

The enormous amount of time, love and money spent on the

house over the years by its previous owners had resulted in

a unique atmosphere, which was instantly recognized by its

new owners — and by Nina. The preservation of that rare

ambience became a major objective of their joint endeavours.

To start with, great care was taken to ensure that the eighteenth-century panelling, present in almost every room, was not only retained but became an essential feature.

When it came to planning colour schemes, Nina was convinced that bringing the colours of the garden into the interior of the house was the answer. Hence, the beautiful flowered chintzes and silks,

offset by plain linens. The budget was relatively tight so it was important to bear in mind the acres of fabric that would be needed for curtaining many windows – a daunting prospect maybe, but an exciting challenge for Nina.

The following pages show how she set about resolving the many problems and the spectacular results she achieved.

Above: With the introduction of brightly printed fabrics, flamboyant needlepoint patterns and a large, colourful Oriental rug, the once gloomy panelled entrance hall takes on a lively and welcoming air.

Walls decorated in a soft maize yellow will
bring a warm glow to any room

HALL

On entering the beautiful and symmetrical hall on my first visit, I was intrigued by the floor with its broad, curiously shaped and tapered boards. I subsequently learned that a previous owner had taken up the original flagstones, moved them to his conservatory, and re-laid the hall floor with coffin lids. (Where he found such a plethora of lids and what happened to the lidless coffins is, alas, not recounted.) Despite their somewhat esoteric beginnings, we decided to keep the floorboards; they certainly have a place in this glorious hall.

combined with the splendid red and blue rug, provide the finishing touches in this welcoming country hall.

A circular table is a wonderful addition to any country hall, provided there is enough space, of course. Here, the mahogany table, covered with plants and books, most definitely takes centre stage.

A brass hanging lamp, picture lights and a pair of converted mahogany candlesticks, topped with simple black shades, cast a good overall light, ideal for both day and night.

All the architectural elements were still in situ: handsome windows flanking the front door; symmetrically placed, pedimented inner doors; and immaculately preserved panelling. However, the panelling did present one modest problem, as dark panelling tends to give a room a mildly gloomy air. In this case, white doors and cornices proved instant enliveners, and with the discovery of a bright French linen fabric with a large floral design for the curtains, we knew we were on the right track. Tapestry, stitched by my client in a pattern similar to the curtains, covers a pair of high-backed chairs – using an identical pattern to the curtains would have been too trite and obvious. The chairs,

MORNING-ROOM

The panelling in the morning-room, which is directly opposite the front door, is painted a soft maize yellow, a wonderfully sunny tone. After all, this is a morning-room, light and bright, with four large windows overlooking the garden – highly decorative features in their own right.

Old-fashioned chintz curtains work well with a plain yellow sofa and two green velvet chairs, embellished with yards of cord, fringe and tassels. Groups of botanical prints with pale green mounts and black frames complement the hand-painted cushions. All in all, the delightful profusion of colour and subtle use of detail that greet guests create an engaging sense of assurance.

Above: In keeping with its proximity to the garden, the morning-room has an overriding botanical theme, from the framed prints and hand-painted cushions to the tulip-shaped porcelain cups.

Drawing-room

There is no evidence of careful and budget-conscious planning in this large, grand and, above all, comfortable room, which is used mostly for entertaining at weekends.

Large drawing-rooms should, ideally, be designed to seat a number of guests, hence the need for chairs that are easily movable, allowing for flexible groupings. That rules out most sofas and heavy armchairs. But have no reservations about introducing well-upholstered stools and benches into the setting. Some chair seats should be firm and a little higher than the average reading chair, say, fourteen to fifteen inches (or some thirty-five centimetres) above carpet level, because many people are uncomfortable in low, squashy chairs. But, equally, there are others who love such yielding chairs, in which they readily doze off, especially after a big dinner. After all, not all guests are performers.

At some point in the history of this house, the drawing-room comprised two rooms, borne out by the impressive reeded columns, now required as load-bearing supports for the upstairs rooms. Marbling the columns in the main colours of the room has diminished what could have been a rather formidable presence.

When my client picked out a fabulously expensive French print for the curtains, I saw problems ahead. There goes my budget, I thought. In such circumstances, it's up to the decorator to come up with a sensible solution that incorporates the wishes of the client yet doesn't send the budget overboard. In this case, my suggestion was to make the curtains in an inexpensive, unlined silk taffeta and use the French print to upholster a pair of French chairs.

This floral print, in fact, formed the basis of the decoration: the curtains have pink, yellow and green stripes; the walls are dragged in three shades of champagne pink; and the sofas are covered with a dusky pink linen. The final vital touch is the Pontromoli needlework rug worked in the most wonderful colours.

As the budget was limited, we invested not in paintings but mirrors and prints, including some Chinese panels in shades of terracotta and green.

Turning this imposing space, which is dominated by the reeded columns, into an informal room for entertaining presented something of a challenge. Shades of soft pink and yellow and the prettiest of floral chintzes were introduced to create a warm atmosphere, while a faux marble finish on the columns makes them appear much less obtrusive.

*D*INING-ROOM

The dining-room – another room with excellent proportions – opens into the hall, while a door at the far end leads into the conservatory and the garden beyond.

Dining-rooms have a tendency to act as stage-sets and need to be ready for 'curtain-up' both during the day *and* at night, so it is important to choose a wall colour that looks good on all occasions. In this instance, we decided on a terracotta/deep rose lacquer, which I call 'flower-pot pink'. This looks particularly good with the terracotta, dark blue and beige carpet and the soft terracotta print on the chairs. It also emphasizes the colours of the oil painting which

hangs above the console table. A set of Piranesi prints, with fountains as their theme, is decoratively grouped either side of the marble fireplace – an original feature of the house.

The room is bathed in natural light by day. For evening light we finally settled on soft, mainly candle, light: gilt and crystal wall sconces, and, on the table, a group of silver candlesticks arranged on mirror glass to add sparkle, glitter and a touch of *Pride and Prejudice* magic.

Dining-rooms smack of tradition. It's here where we tend to display, and even use, objects inherited from previous generations. Grandma's sauce boats may not be to everyone's taste, but if they are decorative, why not show them off?

Above: Shades of terracotta, that most warming and versatile of colours, underpin the decoration of this dining-room.
The 'flower-pot pink' used on the walls helps to deflect attention away from the oversized fireplace.

CONSERVATORY

The conservatory was originally just a wide passage, linking the dining-room to the far end of the house. By moving the exterior wall three feet out (one metre), we were able to create a sunny breakfast room. Rust-coloured split-cane blinds diffuse what can be very strong sunlight on midsummer days. We decided on rust to complement the brick walls and the colours in the adjacent dining-room.

The garden chairs were originally painted white. Stripped and polished, they have now taken on a new lease of life, and by covering them with a rust and stone striped fabric, they are both practical and comfortable.

Above: Shaded from the blazing overhead sun, this conservatory is the perfect location for al fresco entertaining. While the white embroidered tablecloth and fresh flowers add a touch of elegance, the padded cushions tied onto the garden chairs ensure absolute comfort.

Black is probably the most underrated and under-used colour in decorating, even in bedrooms

Main bedroom

At some point in their lives, chintz enthusiasts inevitably fall for the charms of *Roses and Pansies*, an all-time favourite from Colefax & Fowler. My clients had an overwhelming desire to cover their entire bedroom with it: curtains, bed hangings and upholstery.

The generous proportions of the bedroom called for an equally generous curtain treatment, so I used what I term 'Lucinda' drapery – exotic swags with a frilled base, very popular when I first started decorating – for the curtains, pelmets and matching half-tester. I do feel that, nowadays, frills have been rather overdone, but if you have the height and space and can't afford an elaborate fringe, this treatment can prove a useful and budget-conscious alternative.

Black ebonized furniture was the perfect choice to balance a room that was dominated by yards of chintz. Such pieces have the knack of 'anchoring' a room. Pale furniture in this instance would have faded into obscurity. I think a touch of black works in almost every situation, including bathrooms and cloakrooms. Many people have a fear of black. Be brave!

Leading off the bedroom is a small bathroom with cream panelled walls and biscuit-coloured carpet. A small chair by the bath is also covered with the famous *Roses and Pansies* chintz and the walls are lined with a set of floral prints in unusual mirrored frames.

Left: The quintessential English country-house look. Floral chintz curtains and bed drapery, festooned and swagged, lace cushions and a deep-pile carpet spell unashamed luxury.
Right: The floral theme established in the bedroom is carried through to the en suite bathroom, and in the botanical prints there is also an echo of the morning-room. With a splash of colour supplied by the chintz-covered chair, the effect is fresh and undeniably feminine.

Guest bedroom

Along with the rest of the bedrooms, the guest bedroom has panelled walls and four large windows. The walls were already painted white with a pale blue surround, so I chose a delightful blue, pink and white chintz for the curtains and upholstery, which emphasized the existing colours. This decorative scheme from the past had offered me both a challenge and a solution.

For some reason there was a large space between the top of the window and the underside of the cornice (known as the 'deadlight'). To counteract any sense of imbalance, I used an overscaled pelmet, scooped up into rosettes.

By this point in our programme we were getting a trifle low on furniture – and funds! So, when my clients produced a nineteenth-century Rococo-style sleigh-bed covered in gold radiator paint, I took a deep gulp and suggested painting it white. Now, covered with a white crocheted bedspread and criss-cross chintz eiderdown, it is a spectacular and unique piece.

The four large windows mean that the room has plenty of natural light during the day; at night candlestick lights, table lamps and candles create a soft, relaxing mood.

Second guest bedroom

This was the last room we tackled in our decoration programme, and we weren't at all surprised to learn that the budget was threadbare. In such circumstances, improvisation becomes the name of the game.

Working with the room's existing good points, we chose a lovely green and white chintz – an old fern design much favoured by Elsie de Wolfe, which I discovered while researching a book on this legendary American decorator. The problem of what to do with the bare walls was solved by stencilling the fern design onto the panels: small and light at the top of the walls, becoming larger and more intense below the dado rail. The work was beautifully executed by a specialist, and we became so excited by the results that we proceeded to stencil everything that didn't move, including the bedside tables.

To restore a sense of balance to this painted room, we added a serpentine chest-of-drawers made of mahogany. If such treasures could talk, the message would certainly be: never underestimate the power of wood; its colour, richness and warmth can do wonders for any room.

A muslin-covered dressing-table – such a splendid piece of bedroom decoration and, sadly, rather overlooked these days – is laden with an octagonal glass mirror, picture frames, crystal boxes and pretty china lamps. However, we did make sure that there was still enough room for guests to put their weekend paraphernalia.

More than any other room in the house, a guest bedroom should be welcoming. Visitors should be able to close the door behind them and make themselves feel completely at home – temporarily, at least!

Postscript

This is essentially a family home where most of the entertaining takes place at weekends. My aim was to create a warm, comfortable base for my clients, their young family and an influx of guests. After all, half the fun of going away for the weekend is arriving at the house with the sure expectation of having an enjoyable time.

*Far left: With a coat of white paint, the gold sleigh-bed, which had been languishing in the attic,
becomes a romantic and glamorous addition to the guest bedroom. Above: The famous fern chintz decorates the second guest bedroom from
top to toe. By this stage the coffers were empty, but stencilled fern motifs on the wall panels more
than compensate for the lack of prints or paintings.*

CHAPTER 9

ROOFTOP DRAMA

Converting a New York penthouse into a pied à terre for a

French-American couple based in Paris proved to be one of

the most pleasurable of recent commissions for Nina. The

fact that her clients took great interest in the project made it

even more rewarding. Nina was given the task of transforming

three fairly large, but nondescript, reception rooms into a

colourful and comfortable home-from-home, which could be

adapted for entertaining. Fortunately, no structural alterations

were necessary; all the changes that Nina made were cosmetic.

Adjoining rooms without doors create a feeling of space and freedom

RECEPTION ROOMS

Dominated by a window running the full length of one wall, the square entrance hall receives abundant natural light throughout the day. Here, a grand opening leads into the drawing-room. From there, a similar opening reveals the dining-room. In brief, three wonderful rooms, devoid of doors, flowing from one to another.

To emphasize the scale of the door openings, I enlarged the frames with extra mouldings, which resulted in a set of rooms offering the flexibility and freedom of an eighteenth-century enfilade. One of my guidelines is: 'Whatever you do, it should be unexpected.' With that in mind, I set out to design a group of rooms with a central decorative theme using exciting colours and fabrics, together with good European furniture.

HALL

The first thing to be decided upon was which colour to use for the walls. Whatever we chose for the hall would establish the decorative base for this large, but unusually compact, apartment. We eventually settled for a wonderfully rich red, self-stripe wallpaper and matching red taffeta curtains. This must have been the right choice because neither client nor decorator has since cast a single regretful backward glance.

The next step was a rug, and this we discovered while visiting a specialist rug importer from Romania. We were shown a design with huge overblown roses and big leaves. So smitten was my client with this particular rug that she commissioned a series of three for the reception rooms, each with similar designs and colours, but contrasting backgrounds. Inevitably, they became the predominant influence in the overall decorative scheme. Although providing a striking visual link between the three rooms, they still allow the rooms their separate identities.

The rose-patterned theme gave us the opportunity to be bold and dramatic with colour and texture. (Red roses look stunning against black, for example.) By mixing larger and smaller designs, reversing colours and using silks and satins, together with cotton, tapestry and wool, the overall effect is quite theatrical.

As light needed to be reduced rather than emphasized, we decided that we could afford to lose at least one-third of the window space. Generous amounts of taffeta ruched onto a pole with huge upstanding frills, caught up and held back with bows, look sensational. But too much red can be daunting, so I incorporated pretty undercurtains, depicting overblown roses, which can be easily drawn.

Lighting has proved easy. The hall is bathed with natural light during the day and, thanks to borrowed light from the adjoining room, is never dark and rarely even dull. At night, a magnificent enamel and brass chandelier gives a good overall light, while an antique tea caddy lamp, complete with black shade, sheds a pool of soft light from its position in the corner. Black remains the classic balancing colour for red and beige.

The walls are lined with a collection of Piranesi prints, depicting furniture and fireplace designs. Curiously, it was their gold and black frames, which echo the doorway moulding, that inspired me in the first place. They also made me realize that the scheme needed to be anchored with one or two pieces of black furniture, a decorative innovation that had the built-in bonus of playing down any hint of a too-bountiful rose crop.

Left: As the three reception rooms flow one into the other, their decoration needed to establish a sense of continuity, even down to the eccentric metal palm tree in the hall mirroring the living ferns in the drawing-room.

DRAWING-ROOM

Although the colour scheme established in the hall is continued through into the drawing-room, the white base colour of the rug and the thin red stripes on the ticking lining the walls prevent the dark colours from becoming too dominant. On the other hand, a possible wishy-washy effect is avoided by the dark red border running around the edges of the ticking. The rest of the room is what I can only define as a controlled melody of colour, with vibrant red, green and beige tones highlighted with injections of black, gilt and blue.

For the upholstery, I used a gloriously overscaled satin print in red, aquamarine and beige, in conjunction with a small black and rose cotton print, which matches the table-cloth in the hall. The rug, with its huge pink and red roses, works really well with the red ticking and the assortment of prints, checks and tapestries. Frills, cords, tassels and

Above: The colours in the drawing-room achieve a perfect harmony, with the rich red, gold and black balanced by the cooler tones of blue and white china. A medley of patterns and colours can look fabulous, but you must know when to stop. There is a fine line between a room rich in colourful detail, and one that looks too busy and overcrowded. Left: A subtle colour reversal is at play, with the hall's broadly striped dark red walls and black floral rug giving way in the drawing-room to cream wallpaper with thin red stripes and a cream rose-patterned rug.

A bureau-plat, positioned behind the sofa, breaks up the room, creating two separate seating areas: an informal grouping of sofas and chairs around the fire-place, and at the other end of the room, another sofa and a Louis XV chair (see opposite).

throws all complement each other in this wonderful explosion of colour. The final result is a classic example of how the most unlikely colours and fabrics can be fused together successfully.

To create a focal point and introduce a feeling of intimacy in the room, I had wall-to-wall bookcases built either side of the fireplace. My clients invited a specialist painter from France to *faux* marble the fireplace and paint the bookcases, which echo the colours of the walls.

Spacious without being cathedral-like, the drawing-room needed to seat at least ten people at any given time. This it does with accomplished ease. The main seating area is in front of the fireplace, with a large coffee table in the centre and a mahogany and glass screen in one corner, a comfortable arrangement that ensures the room is not *too*

formal. The screen and the ornate ormolu mirror above the fireplace instil light into the room – an important element in any scheme as colourful and glamorous as this. Another smaller seating area is arranged against an inside wall close to the entrance. This area can be quickly enlarged by pulling up a pair of French Louis XV chairs, which are perfect for the purpose. In the centre of the room, a handsome brass-banded bureau-plat, covered with an assortment of objects and a lamp, backs onto a sofa, making the ideal room-break.

Throughout the room, a collection of blue and white china – a favourite accessory of my clients – prevents the predominating reds from becoming overpowering. On brackets, on shelves, and elsewhere, they take the place of paintings and give the room enlivening splashes of colour.

*Mixing and matching colours and fabrics in a room
is enormous fun and can result in highly successful
and original decorative schemes*

DINING-ROOM

The dining-room overlooks an outside well at the rear of the apartment building. This dark and forbidding feature is there for keeps, and there was no apparent way of lessening its gloom. But an old adage was adapted and given up-to-the-minute credence: 'If it's dark, make it darker, but not threatening.' Far from it. With black as the dominant theme, a splendid extravaganza evolved, using strong red, aquamarine and beige fabric on the walls. Neatly bordered with a dark red braid tacked under the red and beige cornice, the decoration links up with that of the adjacent drawing-room.

Most of the furniture is black – that effective foil for red – and designed and made in Paris, since dining-room furniture can prove seriously expensive in New York. We decided to put a portion of the budget towards one really good piece of furniture: a commode. Against the far wall, a black *étagère* echoes the shape of the shelves in

the drawing-room, and a fine eighteenth-century mirror, edged with elaborate gilt decoration, is flanked by a pair of black and gilt sconces.

Dramatic backgrounds need dramatic lighting. In this instance, the effect is heightened with a brilliant crystal and gilt chandelier, suspended above the table, and pretty glass lamps with red silk shades on either side of the console table. On the table a pair of storm lights flicker, adding to the sense of drama.

With so much going on in a room, you can afford to be sparing with paintings, however keen a collector you may be. Here, we have used just two paintings – one on either side of the entrance to the dining-room. More blue and white china provides a link with the adjoining room, preventing the scheme from becoming monotonous.

POSTSCRIPT

What I particularly liked about this commission was my client's enthusiasm and cooperation. At the beginning of the project, we established in one 'no-holds-barred' discussion how the closely related rooms should be decorated. It is a great pleasure when a client is prepared to be so involved – and so obviously enjoys the experience. For the decorator, such commitment is immensely gratifying, especially when both parties are in complete agreement and the client is such fun to work with. Her ideas were bold and imaginative throughout, and, together, we transformed a nondescript New York penthouse into an unexpected and dramatic roof-top eyrie, with versatile seating and adequate room space, ready for all manner of entertaining.

Left: A dining- and drawing-room so close together are perfect
for entertaining, ensuring an effortless after-dinner transition
from the table to the comfortable chairs around the fire.
Right: Light, pale colours would have looked washed out in the
dimly lit dining-room. Reverting to the deeper colours used in the hall
made the room appear warmer, while the blue and white china and
floral fabric continue the themes established in the drawing-room.

CHAPTER 10

TOWN AND COUNTRY

Moving house, the death of a loved one and divorce are

probably the three most disturbing events to occur in anyone's

life. Consider, then, the prospect of moving from a well-loved

but over-large country home to two new residences: a smaller

country house and a large town house.

Such was the situation faced by the couple whose two homes

are shown here. Fortunately, they decided to involve Nina in

the project in its early stages, even providing her with a large

scrapbook that was filled with photographs of their furniture.

The larger and more involved the decorating project, the greater the need for detailed planning

CITYSCAPE

The new London home – a large Victorian double-fronted house – had recently been 'done up' by a property developer with rather dubious taste, who filled it with an over-generous amount of ornate chandeliers, curtains and other furnishings. We all agreed that these should be dispatched to the saleroom as soon as possible.

To begin with, the house seemed too large. Or was it? I started with the drawing-room.

A tall painted cupboard in one corner of the drawing-room provides a lofty display area for a collection of blue and white Chinese pots and ginger jars, as well as being home to two television sets.

DRAWING-ROOM

At the very start of this commission, my clients made it clear that their drawing-room would be used for grand entertaining as well as a retreat for the family where they could relax or watch television. The first step towards accommodating their wishes was to put back the original double doors, which allowed the room to be treated as two spaces or one, depending on the occasion.

One end of the drawing-room has all the appearance of a small, self-sufficient anteroom, pretty but formal, with rather dignified chairs positioned close to the grand piano in the bay window.

The effect at the opposite end of the room is rather less formal, with tempting sofas and a striped wing chair casually, yet invitingly, arranged to create a spacious and comfortable seating area. Here, my client, who is an avid follower of the races, can relax and watch two televisions at the same time. Natural light streams in through the wide bay window, which overlooks the garden and provides a magnificent view.

The drawing-room is exceptional in its ability to play two roles with consummate ease: intimate and cosy for quiet family gatherings, it is also ready for immediate transformation into a spacious room for entertaining.

Divided by double doors, the drawing-room consists of two self-sufficient areas. The more formal end seemed the natural home for a baby grand piano. A casual arrangement of framed family photographs on the piano top, together with injections of bright colour from the flowers and a coral and blue rug, ensure the look is not overly grand.

I based the colours in the room on a pair of needlework rugs in delightful shades of coral, blue and sand, which look perfect with the pale parchment walls, rush matting and damask curtains. By keeping to these basic colours and textures, we were able to use subtle variations at either end of the room without the overall result looking too busy. The best way I know of playing down the grandeur of such overly large rooms is to replace more formal fabrics with colourful prints and bold stripes. These, combined with rougher textures such as needlework jacquard and thick chenille velvet, can make a room look, and feel, more relaxed. It will still look elegant and luxurious, but avoids Versailles-style grandeur.

Introducing my clients' existing furniture into the new decorative scheme was an enjoyable exercise; there were so many wonderful pieces to choose from. Whenever I needed to fill a space, out came the scrapbook and the perfect piece would present itself.

Above the sofa, I placed a collection of paintings and drawings, all by the same artist. The arrangement may look a trifle random at first, but getting the pictures organized was rather like doing a complicated jigsaw puzzle.

Right and above left: Mixing warm tones of brick red, terracotta and coral with blue and yellow helped to create a comfortable, lived-in feel – the accessories did the rest. Paintings, family photographs and colourful china ornaments, along with books and magazines piled high on the coffee table, make the room intimate and comfortable, despite its grand proportions.

The Gothic style of the gilt pelmet board sets the scene for the luxurious curtains. Made of midnight-blue velvet, these are enhanced with their own deep pelmet, trimmed with blue and gold fringing, and edged with a wide border in gold-coloured ottoman and blue and gold cord.

Despite its generous size and attractive architectural features, the dining-room still presented a few decorative problems. For example, the handsome French white marble fireplace was inexplicably off-centre. The solution was to move the dining-table and chairs nearer to the bay window to restore a sense of visual balance.

𝒟INING-ROOM

As the dining-room was to be used primarily at night, we decided to make it really ornate with rich colours and unusual decorative details. I based the theme around a spendid gilded Gothic pelmet board, transferred from my clients' previous home. Re-shaped to fit these dining-room windows, it looks magnificent.

Such a bold start needed to be matched with equally dramatic colours and fabrics. After much deliberation we chose midnight blue – a jewel of a colour, especially at night – for the rich velvet curtains, while navy and gold damask walls provided the perfect background for the paintings and blue and white china. This was exactly the subtle,

sophisticated effect we were after. Or nearly. Too much of one colour, above all dark blue, can be overpowering. A set of ten dining chairs, upholstered in cream, green, navy and gold tapestry, introduced the final yet decisive element in this interplay of unusual colours.

Lighting was planned to enhance and flatter the colour scheme. Midnight blue has a highly idiosyncratic nature, becoming so much deeper and more mysterious by night, and reflections in the mirror glass magnify the effect. Wall sconces emulate candles; a pair of table lamps stand on the sideboard; and two handsome blackamoors on black reeded columns present their trays of candles. All make their individual contributions to the elegance of the scene.

Left: Decorating a small room demands a bold approach. I chose a dramatic scheme of red, white and black for the cloakroom, accented with a gilt mirror frame and wall sconces.

Cloakroom

The smallest room in the house is too often regarded as the least interesting, despite the amenities it offers. That certainly isn't the case here. This cloakroom has mahogany panels to dado height and a cream marble basin surround. This was a room clearly yearning for an injection of colour. Red lacquer walls, red, black and tan checked blinds and a set of animal paintings from the owners' collection met that need. As well as being a decorative feature in its own right, the overscaled mirror makes the room appear much larger than it actually is.

Master bedroom

The house was, fortunately, large enough for my clients to convert an entire floor into their private suite of rooms.

Originally gloomy and dark green, the bedroom nevertheless had splendid proportions, with a handsome fireplace and large bay windows overlooking the garden. By choosing a colour theme of soft blue and white, we succeeded in creating an overall effect of restfulness and tranquillity. The unusually shaped headboard is piped and buttoned in blue to complement the fringe on the half-tester and bed curtains. (Half-testers are particularly attractive, especially those that extend to the full width of the bed. They are nowhere near as daunting as four-posters or as negligible as half-coronas.)

By cutting the cornices back from above the windows, we were able to fix the gathered pelmet on to the ceiling. This meant that we could still have a generous pelmet and allow maximum light to filter into the room. The curtains, in the same blue and white fabric as the walls, half-tester and bed valance, are generous, with the pelmet fringed in cream as a contrast to the blue fringe on the tester.

ʙᴀᴛʜʀᴏᴏᴍ

The furniture in the adjoining bathroom is free-standing. When you have adequate space, those so-called labour- and space-saving built-in units are unnecessary. Here, too, a charming blue and white fabric has been used on the walls and for the curtains. The scale of the design is the same as that of the bedroom, which creates a pleasing sense of unity and links the whole en suite effect.

ᴘᴏsᴛsᴄʀɪᴘᴛ

I was determined to make this London home as comfortable for my clients as their more spacious house in the country from which they had just moved. In giving the house a rambling, country-house feel, the move was relatively pain-less, and the family is well and truly settled in.

Now, let's go to the country...

Conventional bedside tables were replaced by two mismatching chests-of-drawers: perfect for storage and offering far more surface space for lamps, books and a telephone. I often wonder why this arrangement isn't followed more widely; standard bedside tables can be pretty but often prove inadequate. The chests can be different widths, but should be the same height, or the lamps will look out of balance.

Above left and above: Pieces of furniture above and beyond the necessities will make bedrooms and bathrooms even more comfortable. In the bedroom a sofa, covered in white chenille velvet, faces the fireplace, offering a cosy spot for cold winter nights. In the adjoining bathroom, white cupboards resembling French armoires, a pretty painted bookcase displaying a collection of books and scent bottles, and a dressing-table and chair help to create a truly relaxing retreat.

With a little visual trickery and decorator know-how,
even the most awkwardly shaped and unpleasing
rooms can be transformed

Above: Originally an unpromising, tunnel-like space, the hall is now comfortable and inviting. To counter the problem of the
low ceiling, I gave the curtains arched pelmets which create an impression of height. Right: A tantalizing glimpse of the bar, through
a Victorian Gothic archway, reveals olive green walls and rich mahogany fittings.

Country setting

My clients were already the owners of this nineteenth-century stable complex, which functioned as a working stable and a venue for meetings, and included a vast kitchen catering for the jockeys and stable hands. My brief was to convert part of it into a country house.

The shape of the stable block, which was built around a courtyard, was somewhat unpromising: long and narrow with low ceilings that seemed to stretch forever. Upstairs, a rabbit warren of pokey offices obviously required a number of alterations to transform it into comfortable bed-rooms and bathrooms. With the help of an imaginative architect, we set about the task in hand.

Hall

A stone lobby with double glass-panelled doors leads into the hall. Today visitors are instantly struck by its warmth and cosiness, quite a magical transformation from the awkwardly shaped and unwelcoming hall that confronted me on my first visit. In many ways, this was the most important area to get right because a hall, whatever its spatial shortcomings, sets the scene for the rest of the house. The major structural change we made was building a completely new staircase, which helped enormously in making the hall practical and inviting.

We based our colour scheme on an extremely expensive Italian linen, with bright red flowers and lots of light and dark mossy greens, for the curtains. We did try to find a cheaper alternative but to no avail. To balance the budget, we then found an inexpensive wallpaper with a lovely soft green design, thick enough to conceal the copious small, but nonetheless irritating, defects on the walls beneath. We hung it up the front stairs, along the corridors and down the back stairs. This gave a sense of unity to the house, which seemed to open up as we went.

When the moment came to unroll the large nineteenth-century rug, my heart skipped a beat. The colours were wonderful, echoing those of the wallpaper and curtain fabric. Yet, although mixing lots of patterns and colours is a thrilling experience, I felt that these needed one solid colour to pull them together. I decided to use a dark green striped fabric on the Charles II high-backed chairs. The effect was dramatically right.

If you are lucky enough to have a large square or rectangular hall, there is no doubt at all that a round table in the centre is the most aesthetically pleasing and effective of all furniture arrangements. A welcoming fire in the huge stone fireplace warms limbs and gladdens the eye, as well as diminishing the rather cold and austere effect of the flagstone floor. A wooden screen, covered in old prints, conceals the stairway and, more importantly, gives a sense of privacy to the hall.

One of the problems we faced was where to house the owner's very large collection of trophies and bronzes. The answer was simple. Bearing in mind that any room benefits from one over-scaled piece of furniture, we consulted the scrapbook. There we found an immensely impressive glazed breakfront bookcase: the perfect home for treasured possessions.

Bar

The aim here was to create a convivial drinking halt, complete with authentic mahogany counter, high stools and, of course, juke box. Located between the drawing-room and the hall, the bar is ready-made for conversation and large enough to accommodate around twenty people (standing room only, of course). Olive green walls, a comfortable sofa and chairs and green linen curtains, high-lighted by a pair of Gothic giltwood mirrors, complete this traditional and cosy retreat.

Short of bringing in the bulldozers, colour is the most effective
way of widening a space

DRAWING-ROOM

Initially, the 'corridor effect' made the drawing-room seem decidedly narrower than it really is, a visual defect not helped by the strange, inverted ceiling with its extra moulding, which added to the pronounced recessed look.

The bookcase, which was already in place at the far end of the drawing-room, did, in part, succeed in making the room appear wider, and, consequently, shorter. However, the overall effect was marred by mirror in the centre of the bookcase, which divided it in two. By removing the mirror and continuing the shelves right across the room, the threatened tunnel look disappeared completely.

The fireplace was oversized in comparison with the windows, which were of different sizes anyway, though this need not be a great drawback in a drawing-room. By making all the curtains to the same design and scale, the windows now appear to be of the same height, helping to create that sense of unity I wanted to achieve.

The walls are covered with a cream damask wallpaper, which creates a depth of colour that is impossible to achieve with paint. Simple, natural linen curtains and an olive green, red and rust linen print on one sofa complement the rich red of the velvet-covered sofa, which I 'inherited' from my clients' scrapbook.

Above: I had to take care that the furniture arrangement in the drawing-room didn't emphasize its corridor-like proportions. Placing a pair of two-seater sofas to either side of the fireplace helped to break up the room and make it look wider.

Right: A trompe l'oeil door, skilfully concealed within the bookshelves, leads to a stairway to the guest bedrooms.

Featuring a large bay window overlooking the gardens, the dining-room is used predominantly for daytime meals rather than evening entertaining. I therefore decided to keep the decoration simple, emphasizing the room's light and airy qualities with pale colours. Although the same floral pattern is repeated on both walls and curtains, the overall effect is one of lightness and delicacy.

Seating in the drawing-room posed something of a problem. Whatever I did seemed to emphasize the 'corridor effect', added to which the wall opposite the fireplace was not long enough for a sofa. The age-old alternative solution was a pair of overscaled two-seater sofas on either side of the fireplace with a large upholstered stool holding centre stage. This arrangement makes the room look wider and certainly extremely cosy.

Picture lights positioned above the paintings provide a soft background glow, enhanced by table lamps dotted around the room, all controlled by dimmer switches.

Oil paintings and bronzes of the owner's various horses enliven the walls and display surfaces.

Dining-room

We all felt that this dining-room should be quite different from that in the London home, so I made it light and bright using pretty colours and simple drapery.

We needed a fabric that would complement the dining-room chairs, which were already covered in a rust chenille. After considering several wallpapers, even a mural, we found the perfect Adam-style fabric to use for both the walls and curtains. The latter, with their generously ruched pelmet, decorated with a rust cord running along the top and a rust bobble fringe around the base, are surprisingly successful.

Background lighting comes from a pair of lamps on the sideboard and also from picture lights.

ℬedroom

In the master bedroom I chose a cream damask fabric for the walls and curtains. I was rather apprehensive about using this material at first because it wasn't the best quality, but it was good looking and incredibly cheap; nobody was likely to spot the near-invisible imperfections.

By using the same beautiful damask for the tester, bedhangings, valance and curtains, together with a little cream lace, the room looks wonderfully luxurious. The addition of lace softens the overall effect as well as complementing the pile of lace cushions and the beautiful hand-embroidered bed-cover.

Above: A predominantly cream colour scheme has a simple elegance and can be relied upon to create a luxurious look. Dark wood furniture and touches of black were added to prevent the scheme looking washed-out and insipid. Above right: The two chairs flanking the windows are upholstered in an antique needlepoint fabric, which mirrors the colours of the garden beyond.

As the bathroom window overlooks the stable yard, it was important to consider the need for privacy. Generous lace draperies, with bobble fringing, and a pull-down blind guarantee seclusion, whilst allowing a gentle light to filter through on sunny days.

*P*OSTSCRIPT

The brief from my clients was simple and straightforward: to decorate their unusual country house to their satisfaction within the given budget. Happily, it was achieved, and the experience was made even more pleasurable by working with clients who so obviously enjoy decorating.

This is a practical house; it works well and is extremely comfortable. More importantly, we managed to exorcise the overwhelmingly claustrophobic effect of the narrow, never-ending first view of the interior. Now, first impressions are infinitely improved.

The two windows that butt up against each other needed careful consideration, but one set of curtains and a pelmet running right across the top solved the problem. The curtains are simple, yet full, with gathered ruched headings and linen fringes at the base. Plain holland blinds, which prevent sunlight damaging the furniture, are also enlivened with a linen edging.

*B*ATHROOM

There are two bathrooms: one is a simple, fit-for-its-purpose retreat; the other, illustrated here, is the complete opposite and outrageously feminine. In the latter, a staircase originally dominated one corner. After its removal, the space seemed almost too large, so we introduced a small stone fireplace and armoire-style cupboards, with wire panels lined with cream fabric, and a comfortable sofa – additions guaranteed to enhance the air of femininity.

Above right: The bathroom features another cream scheme, this time with an ultra-feminine twist. The lavish lace draperies, which are edged with bobble fringing, and a coordinating pull-down blind provide privacy, yet allow the sunlight to filter through.

CHAPTER 11

ELEGANCE IN MINIATURE

During the early part of her career, Nina was given the chance

to decorate the private apartments of a stately home. She

had access to the attic, which was crammed with untold

treasures and from which she could select whatever she needed.

Twenty-five years later, Nina was asked to decorate

the dower house, to which her client had moved, passing

the main house into the care of her son and his family.

Situated in the grounds of the stately home, the dower

house is a Queen Anne gem, blessed with perfect proportions.

When moving to a smaller home, edit your possessions carefully so that you look forwards with enjoyment and not backwards with regret

Thanks to a major overhaul by my client's parents in the 1960s, the dower house is far more spacious inside than could possibly be guessed from the outside. In a sense, its decorative scheme was already established when I took on the commission: there was a great deal of furniture of the right scale that already belonged to the house, although it had, over the years, deteriorated and was in need of repair and restoration. However, my client did make some additions with pieces she already owned and treasured.

Moving from an exceedingly large house into something far smaller means adjustments at every stage. My advice to anyone having to reduce the size of their home is simple: take only the possessions that you really love.

I wanted to preserve certain fabrics and wallpapers that illustrated the taste and flair of my client's mother who had last decorated the house. She, too, knew instinctively that bold, rich colours were the key to the decoration.

HALL

On entering the house one is immediately aware of what I term the 'visual warmth' of the hall and the rooms leading off it. To the right is the dining-room and to the left the study. As my aim was to create the effect of an enfilade of rooms with the hall at the centre, I chose colours that would help to give the impression of a series of rooms flowing one into the other.

If you decide to make an especially bold statement with colour, start as you mean to carry on. The hall, which is lined with a striking, red floral-patterned wallpaper on a stone background, certainly sets the pace for the rest of the decorative scheme.

The existing dado rail was stencilled with a cord and tassel motif for additional interest. Taupe wool carpet here, and throughout the house, proves, as always, that it is the perfect background for almost any colour and texture.

DINING-ROOM

The dining-room is dominated by a bold red and cream striped wallpaper and plain red curtains. The pelmets, trimmed with cord and fringe, are fixed as high as possible above the window to give height to the room. This also means that as little light as possible is blocked out by the pelmet. Guests are frequently bowled over by the strength of the stripes in this little room and openly voice their intentions to create the same look in their own homes.

It was important to have a dining-table that would accommodate eight guests comfortably, and even more important to ensure that it was the right shape and size for

Left: Taking a bold approach to the decoration created an elegant enfilade of rooms: broad red and white stripes in the dining-room, richly patterned walls in the hall and golden-yellow wallpaper in the drawing-room.

*Left: The dining-room table
has been the focal point of
this room for many years. Just
the right size for this tiny,
doll's house dining-room, it will
seat eight comfortably.
Below: The stunning raspberry-
red curtains introduce an
element of grandeur – albeit on
a reduced scale. Fixing the
pelmet as high as possible
made the small window
appear much taller.*

the proportions of the room. Fortunately, an oval wooden table with a green marbleized top was already in place. My client's mother had originally bought it in the 1930s for a much narrower room, but on moving house she found the table simply wasn't large enough for the number of guests she wished to entertain. To overcome the problem, she added extensions to it and employed a specialist paint finisher to marble it in green malachite. The table now seats eight, and is perfect for the room.

We were also lucky to have a delightful set of chairs, which simply needed re-upholstering. We settled on a tapestry material in green, red and stone for the fronts of the chairs and a simple checked fabric for the backs.

To make the room even cosier, mirrors and paintings line the walls, while a corner table is covered with a collection of green glass and candlesticks.

DRAWING-ROOM

The drawing-room, an extension added in the 1960s, is a sunny, south-facing room with spectacular views over the garden. The colour to use for its decoration seemed obvious: yellow, with yellow-on-yellow striped wallpaper and a bold yellow and blue patterned fabric for the curtains. Paintings, pieces of china, cushions and lampshades introduce dashes of contrasting colour.

My client wished to be able to seat ten people comfortably in the drawing-room, but this did pose rather a problem in such a small space. However, the combination of a small two-seater sofa and a larger three-seater, plus one or two occasional chairs and a comfortable fireside armchair, has proved more than adequate.

The double doors leading into the garden are flanked by pretty circular windows. During the summer months, these are left completely unadorned, allowing uninterrupted views of the garden beyond. In winter, circular wooden boards, painted with *trompe l'oeil* country scenes, cover the windows. As well as helping to conserve the heat, they are highly decorative features in their own right.

Left: The unusual wedge shape of the drawing-room presented a few decorative problems. To detract from its odd proportions, I gave the room a sense of unity by using colours and textures that naturally harmonize and complement each other. Restoring damaged items of family furniture to their former glory was a rewarding challenge; the rich woods look stunning against the yellow walls. Above: The two-seater sofa is covered in the same fabric used for the curtains, seen reflected in the mirror above.

As there was only one large
window in the drawing-room,
we could afford to splash out on
a fabulous pair of curtains. Made
from a blue and yellow floral
damask, handsomely swagged
and fringed, the curtains are
beautifully set off by a striped
under-pelmet. The unusual
round window is one of a pair.
Left bare in summer, they are
covered with decorative boards
during the winter.

MASTER BEDROOM

As this room is so light and airy, I decided to create an uncluttered look with simple furniture and accessories: green, yellow and white chintz fabric, a crisp white cotton bedspread and simple green and white trellis wallpaper.

A charming fireside chair, covered in chintz, introduces a touch of cosiness and warmth, and an antique walnut chest-of-drawers acts as a bedside table. A collection of watercolours and prints on the walls and china on the mantelpiece provide the finishing touches.

Above: The decoration of the master bedroom illustrates one of my decorating maxims: 'Make a light room lighter.' A pale, trellis-patterned wallpaper and a delicate floral chintz create a fresh, country-cottage look that is enhanced by the wooden beams. We were fortunate in that the room already possessed a handsome white fireplace – all the more striking, in my opinion, for its pared-down, plain design. Right: A walnut chest-of-drawers is home to an antique apothecary's chest inlaid with mother-of-pearl, and a lamp with a base converted from a Sèvres vase.

Left: The guest bedroom already featured a wonderful dove grey and pink chintz. Reluctant to throw it out, I had it made into a blind and matching curtains. The miniature armoire beneath houses a collection of beautiful porcelain cups and saucers in complementary colours.

Above: In marked contrast to the master bedroom, the adjoining bathroom is richly patterned. A trompe l'oeil floral wallpaper, resembling gathered fabric, and matching curtains envelop the tiny space and make this the cosiest of retreats.

The pretty chintz wallpaper in the bathroom adjoining the guest bedroom was another original feature. It gave the bathroom a 1930s-style charm, which was further enhanced by fitting a mirrored splashback (backsplash) behind the bath and a pair of pink and white striped taffeta curtains.

ℬATHROOM

My client had fallen hopelessly in love with a rather luxurious-looking American wallpaper, which resembled gathered fabric, strewn with flowers. Since the bathroom was small, we decided we could use it throughout without it being too overwhelming, and have curtains to match. A nineteenth-century boudoir is the end result.

The bath slots neatly into an existing alcove, while extra storage space has been created beneath the basin by building in wooden cupboards.

𝒢UEST BEDROOM SUITE

The best way to accentuate the qualities of an attic room is to emphasize a sense of warmth and cosiness. In the guest bedroom, the dusky pink walls and sill-length curtains in grey and pink chintz, with a matching pull-down blind, create this effect convincingly.

Probably my favourite room in the whole house is the guest bathroom as it has, for me, a real sentimental attachment to the past. The old-fashioned, grey and pink chintzy wallpaper, decorated with roses, arches and lovers, had been introduced by my client's mother. It was so delightful that I felt we had to keep it. The paper was slightly damaged in places, mostly around the windows, but we managed to conceal these areas behind the curtains. Thanks to a plumber who possessed the skills of a master surgeon, the new bathroom equipment was installed with minimal loss of wallpaper. As the original curtains were not worth keeping, we used a pink and white striped taffeta. The overall effect is engagingly romantic.

𝒫OSTSCRIPT

From the start of this commission my aim was to provide as near-perfect a background for my client's existing furniture and possessions as I could. The result is a comfortable house that works well when my client is on her own or when surrounded by guests. I must say that it is immensely rewarding to see the owner of a home happily ensconced in new surroundings that owe something to one's own notions of design and decoration.

CHAPTER 12

DECORATOR TIPS
THE FINISHING TOUCHES

Finishing touches can make a world of difference to a decorative scheme, transforming even the most uninspiring room into somewhere original and exciting. Sharing her decorating wisdom, Nina gives simple but effective tips for making the most of table decorations, cushions, curtains, lighting, bed drapery and display.

RIGHT: An elegant and luxurious table setting, with ruby red glasses and gleaming silverware, creates a wonderful sense of occasion. The spectacular flower arrangements are tall enough not to obscure the guests' views of each other, and, thanks to the room's high ceiling, they never overwhelm.

ABOVE AND RIGHT: Informal al fresco lunches allow you to introduce elements of fun such as a twig place mat, pea-pod napkin ring and folded napkin 'boots'.

TABLE DECORATIONS

Always decorate your table according to the sense of occasion. If it's a lighthearted affair, then the decoration should reflect this, but if the occasion is formal, the table setting should be formal too, even if there are just two of you and you feel like dressing up. There need be no limits to your imagination when it comes to table decoration; what matters is that it gives pleasure to you and, of course, to your guests, who will feel particularly welcome if they're greeted by a table setting that appears tailor-made for them.

● On cold, wet nights a red damask tablecloth will make everyone feel that much cosier. Equally, if it's a hot night, lower the temperature with lighter fabrics in cool colours.

- Sheets make ideal tablecloths because of their size. You can also use upholstery or dress fabric.
- If you're entertaining a lot of people around a collection of odd, round tables, link the tables visually by using similar tablecloths, or establishing a decorative theme.
- For more informal gatherings or entertaining outdoors, paper napkins and tablecloths are fun, attractive, cheap and, of course, disposable.
- It really doesn't matter if your china doesn't match as long as you try to keep to certain colour groups and patterns. It's fun adding to your collection over the years with antique-shop finds.
- To those who take their wines seriously, offer only clear, and preferably thin, glasses, especially if red wines are being served. (Red wine in a coloured glass looks like hemlock!) But that doesn't mean you can't have coloured glasses for water, which will add extra colour to the table.
- Candles and candlesticks are always a delight. On intimate occasions, use low candles to draw the eyes down; in a more convivial atmosphere, mix high and low. The same applies to flowers.
- If you have a glass, marble or wooden table, it's a good idea to have table mats, as they soften the often disruptive noise that's made every time somebody puts down a glass or knife and fork.
- I sometimes take china ornaments off the shelves and add them to the table, or scatter sugared almonds – whatever suits the occasion.

A dining-table can act as a showcase for a treasured collection of china or glassware. This table, usually decorated in informal summery blues and whites, has been transformed into a glamorous backdrop for the fabulous amethyst glassware. Damask napkins and cream Wedgwood plates with an amethyst floral design pick up the colour tones.

RIGHT: Cushions can be made from almost any fabric: this turquoise pair was fashioned from a beaded tea cosy. Cushions of such delicate fabrics are more suited to a bedroom or side chairs than a well-used sofa where they are likely to take rather a beating.

I have unearthed some wonderful cushions and trimmings in antique shops. The strip of antique needlework on the green velvet cushion showing a bee and a lion's head was the inspiration for my 'Lord Lyon' fabric, although the lion's mouth was altered to make him look less fierce. The heraldic cushion beneath needed only rebacking and retrimming to look as good as new. Both these cushions would look marvellous on patterned or plain covers.

Cushions

I think of cushions as the decorative equivalent of eye make-up, as they bring extra colour and drama to a room once it has been decorated. Waiting until the decoration is complete before choosing cushions is sensible because you will then know what colours and textures will work, and there may be some leftover curtain or upholstery fabric you can make use of.

- If you have set your heart on a very expensive fabric but can't afford to use it on a grand scale, cover the cushions with it instead. Backing the cushions with a cheaper, contrasting material will keep the cost down still more.
- Deciding what cushions to use on busy covers can be problematic. A bold chintz cover teamed with cushions in the same fabric looks effective, as do cushions in textured fabrics in plain colours, perhaps with ruched trimmings. But try to avoid an unimaginative 'mix-and-match' look; customizing cushions with, say, scraps of beading or needlework will offset this.
- Cushions in contrasting busy designs can be grouped together, but only if placed on plain sofa- or chair-covers.

- Provided you have good cushion pads in the first place, re-covering cushions can really revitalize a room, and at little cost. I like to have a summer and winter set of covers – bright red checks for the summer, perhaps, and a more luxurious, textured fabric for winter.

- Don't sacrifice practicality for style; a sofa with too many cushions simply isn't comfortable.
- It is all too easy to spend a lot more than you expect on cushion trimmings. Bear in mind that for a 20in (50cm) square cushion you will need more than 2yd (about 2m) of fringe.
- Buttoned cushions can look handsome, but only if expertly made. If you're not a dab hand at buttonholes, don't even consider it.
- Minimum maintenance is of vital importance. Cushion ties may look charming but I certainly don't want to spend a well-earned half-hour of relaxation retying bows.
- Don't restrict yourself to furnishing fabrics: silks, taffetas and dress fabrics are all possibilities. Quilting will help strengthen delicate fabrics.

RIGHT: This assortment of cushions shows what a wealth of different trimmings – from bobble fringes and gathered frills to piping – can be added to create a luxurious finish.

LEFT: Don't be nervous about mixing cushions of different shapes, sizes and textures. Here, cushions in mainly blue and white fabrics – a Paisley, stripe, plaid, toile de Jouy, and a tiny, all-over 'busy' pattern – sit happily side by side, although I wouldn't suggest you have quite so many on a sofa! I always think of the cushion with its little tufts as a 'therapy' cushion – somebody is bound to fiddle abstractedly with the tufts and pull them off!

BELOW: *For an even
more luxurious effect,
consider double-tassel
tie-backs over singles.*

LEFT: *This pair of
unlined lace curtains,
with a bobble-fringe
edging and underblind in
a fabric of the same
design, are undeniably
feminine without being
too frou-frou.*
BELOW LEFT: *By placing
the pelmet high up so
that the fringe just covers
the window frame, this
small window appears
more elegant and lets in
as much light as possible.*

CURTAINS

After deciding on your furniture and paintings,
choosing your curtains is probably the most
important and expensive decorative decision you
will make. Although the proportions of a room
dictate what sort of treatment you should have,
curtains should always be luxurious; fortunately,
there are ways of making them less expensive
than they appear. Although curtains are a major
feature in any room, it is important to realize that
they are not always the *dominant* feature and may
need to take a back seat.

- If you have a tall picture window and low ceiling,
  avoid a wide, repetitive swagged pelmet; it will
  make the window look over-decorated.
- In rooms with high ceilings, allow the curtain to
  tumble onto the floor for a luxurious look.
- It is far better to dress up a small window than
  give it a skimpy curtain. Make sure the curtains
  draw right back for maximum light.

- If your window looks out onto a wonderful view, you won't need screening curtains or sheers. A less pleasant outlook can be obscured with sheers, laces or linens, or perhaps an undercurtain of unlined taffeta, which allows the light to filter through and shows the fabric to best advantage.
- Always err on the generous side with both curtain fabric and headings.
- When planning short pelmets, take into account the fabric pattern. If it's very large, you'll end up chopping off the design in its prime.
- Buying seconds is a good economy measure. Very often the only reason a fabric is a second is because the colours don't meet the standards of the pattern book. Be sure to buy enough; you may not be able to get any more. Most large fabric houses have sales once a year.

- Never choose a curtain fabric from a small sample. It's far better to buy a yard (metre), gather it up and see how it takes the light.
- Don't overlook the backs of fabrics; they may be more attractive than the fronts.
- Wools of any sort drape beautifully.
- Detailing is what separates ordinary curtains from really marvellous ones. If you have a curtain treatment in three colours of chintz, use one colour to bind the curtain and pipe the cushions. Or, if you have chosen a striped fabric for your upholstery, you could cut out strips of the same material and sew them to the leading edge and bottom of the curtains for a cheap and effective result.
- Blinds or wooden shutters, which give a cooler, cleaner look, are perfect in rooms where curtains would look too fussy.

An ormolu hold-back is just one alternative to the more conventional cord or tassel treatment.

ABOVE: A pull-down blind can be an effective addition to curtains if you wish to block out an oppressive sky or unpleasant view without losing too much light.

RIGHT: At night, drawing only the undercurtain, which is in a lighter, contrasting fabric to the main curtain and walls, prevents any feeling of claustrophobia.

DISPLAY

When it comes to display, the first thing that probably springs to mind is pictures, and hanging pictures seems to cause more than a few decorative headaches. But whatever you display – pictures, photographs, mementoes or flowers – all that's needed is a little planning and forethought.

- There are no set rules to picture display; it is all a question of balance. I always arrange pictures in groups on the floor first, then take a deep breath before hanging them. If your measurements are wrong, you will run out of wall space and have pictures left over (I speak from bitter experience), so if you can find somebody else to hang them up for you, better still

- I like to have not more than 2in (5cm) between pictures if they're in a group. I'm also fond of

FAR LEFT: A scallop-edged wallpaper border makes a decorative feature of kitchen shelves.
BELOW LEFT: This collection of tortoiseshell and mother-of-pearl objects is strong enough to stand out against a floral linen tablecloth.
BELOW RIGHT: An intriguing trompe l'oeil effect is created by pasting prints onto the cupboard doors to surround the framed picture.

mixing different types of picture together; sometimes a small oil popped in amongst some prints and watercolours works extremely well, although placing it slightly off-centre within the group is better than in the middle.

- I don't know why, but a slightly larger picture always seems to look better hanging above a smaller picture.

- If you have a collection of similar pictures, perhaps all by the same artist or all black and white, you can prevent the scheme from becoming monotonous by framing them slightly differently and by using different coloured mounts.

- For table display, grouping objects into types is particularly effective – for example, pieces of tortoiseshell, or tortoiseshell combined with mother-of-pearl, bronzes or ormulu. Everything should be arranged in some sort of order, otherwise the display will end up looking messy and uncared for.

- There's nothing nicer than a small table laden with photographs, but avoid having too many different types of frame.

- It's important not to let the background compete with the objects on display. Small silver ornaments look wonderful on a plain colour, such as a plain chenille cloth, but they would have to fight for survival on a chintz background.

- It doesn't matter what you collect as long as you enjoy it; be as eccentric as you like. But remember that as you add to your collection, for reasons of space you will have to edit it.

- Fresh flowers are a wonderful addition to any room, introducing colour as well as creating a welcoming atmosphere. But don't overdo it and make the room resemble a funeral parlour. As I never have the time to fuss with flower arrangements, tulips have become a firm favourite – they virtually arrange themselves.

- There is always a case for dried flowers, especially in homes where people are away frequently but like to be greeted by flowers on their return.

- Dried flowers are inexpensive compared with fresh flowers, but there's nothing more depressing and unkempt than faded and dusty blooms. They are meant to be disposable, so don't feel guilty about throwing them out when they're past their best.

If you don't have many pictures, it is always better to group them on one wall rather than have them dotted around, one on each wall, where they will look insignificant.

LEFT: The gathered
chiffon shade on this
painted antique tea caddy
is lined in pink to cast a
flattering light. The
shade is closed in at the
top so that the light is
directed downwards.
RIGHT: This antique
library light, with brass
legs and mahogany
shelves, manages to be
both attractive and func-
tional. The pleated silk
shade is square to match
the shape of the table.

Lighting

There's no denying it: lighting is not easy and if
you don't plan it carefully enough, a lighting
scheme may ruin the appearance of an otherwise
perfectly decorated room. Its effects can be
varied, from soft and subtle for relaxing evenings
to focused and practical for reading by.

- A mixture of lamps in a room is far more interesting than lamps all of the same design.
- Remember that choosing the right lampshade is
  even more difficult than finding the right base,
  and you may wish to have a shade made to your
  exact requirements.
- Be imaginative. All sorts of objects can be adapted
  into lamp bases.
- Vary the textures and fabrics of the shades – use
  gathered silk, pleats, or a fabric that is used elsewhere in the room.

*The tassel and shells are
an unusual and pretty
addition to this ormolu
lamp with its scalloped
chintz shade. Because
of its fragility, the lamp
would be perfect for a
bedroom dressing-table.*

LEFT: I found this lamp
in Paris and simply
couldn't resist it. It has
an elegant metal stem
and leaves on a square
base and a tiny blue glass
shade. Although modern
in style, it would fit into
almost any interior.

Unusual beaded candle shades teamed with glass bases look stunning at night on the dining-table when the candles are lit. The bobèches (dishes to catch the candle drips), decorated with delightful cherubs and enormous crystal drops, add to the sense of occasion.

● Spotlights do have their place, but position them with care. They are useful in rooms where a lot of light is needed during the day or for tasks in awkward places such as cleaning. For the evenings there should be an alternative, more glamorous lighting scheme.

● Recessed lighting is perfect for small rooms such as cloakrooms and kitchens where dangling light fittings would be obtrusive.

● I place small arm lights inside bed drapery, so there is a practical light for reading by at night. There is then no need to fumble for the switch when you want to go to sleep.

● Lights attached to bookcases in libraries or studies are a useful addition, allowing you to browse through the shelves without squinting.

● Don't overlook the obvious: have as many light sockets as possible in a room.

This eclectic trio of lamps, with leaves as the common theme, are good-looking, practical and will inject a touch of wit into any lighting scheme.

● Lamps should fit comfortably on a table. When buying a base, remember that the overall height will be much greater once a shade has been added. If a lamp is to be used for reading by and is too tall, the bare bulb will shine down into your face and the workings of the lamp will be all too clearly visible.

● If you need a short lampshade but want to give the effect of it being deeper, add a fringe to the bottom. This will also help soften the light.

● If your lampshade is of a light fabric, make sure it is opaque enough to hide the bulb from view.

● Dark lampshades throw the light down and create a more intimate feel.

● As overhead lighting tends to be harsh, incorporate dimmer switches. Small French candle bulbs in chandeliers will cast a softer light.

● Mirrors lining the walls between windows and fitted with candlestick lights or real candles create a romantic mood at night.

For this ceramic urn, one of a pair that I turned into lamps, I chose a dark green shade to complement the dark green velvet sofa; a white shade would have looked too light on top of the black base and would not have fitted in with the dark furniture.

ℬED DRAPERY

Bed drapery is, to a certain extent, everyone's dream, or rather every woman's dream and every man's nightmare. The drapery you choose will depend on the style of the bed and the room. It will add a feeling of either cosiness or luxury, but while drapery should always be shamelessly sumptuous, it doesn't have to be overwhelming.

- There are so many different ways to work with bed drapery. One is to have the outer curtain in the same fabric as the window curtain, with the inner curtain in a contrasting fabric, perhaps muslin or lace. As a general rule, I favour using the same fabric for the outer curtain, bed valance and headboard.

- A corona looks wonderful over a single or double bed but it is simply too small for a king-size bed. For a bed of this size or larger, it's better to keep to a half-tester (really half a four-poster) which gives a better sense of proportion.

- Be sure not to introduce too many materials and trimmings. All you need is an outer fabric, an inner fabric and possibly a simple trimming – certainly nothing too elaborate or you will end up feeling claustrophobic.

- A flattering colour for the inner curtain is essential as that's the colour you will been seen against in the mornings. Yellow is probably the least flattering colour, but if you must have it, use a floral print with yellow in it.

FAR LEFT: Classic but simple curtaining draped over a centrally placed rod creates a splendid backdrop to a French lit-bateau or day-bed. The outer curtain is a plain red linen while the lining is a contrasting red and white cotton print.

LEFT: Simple white muslin drapery looks very pretty and young on this half-tester bed. However, muslin must be kept sparklingly clean, which means washing the drapery at least every three months. Even if the muslin is pre-shrunk, make the drapery slightly on the long side to allow for further shrinkage.

LEFT: Covering the walls, headboard and inner curtain in matching fabric gives a more coordinated look to this room, while using the same ivory fabric for the outside of the corona and the window curtain accentuates the light and airy feel. Small lights inserted through the drapery allow for reading at night.

$\mathcal{I}$NDEX

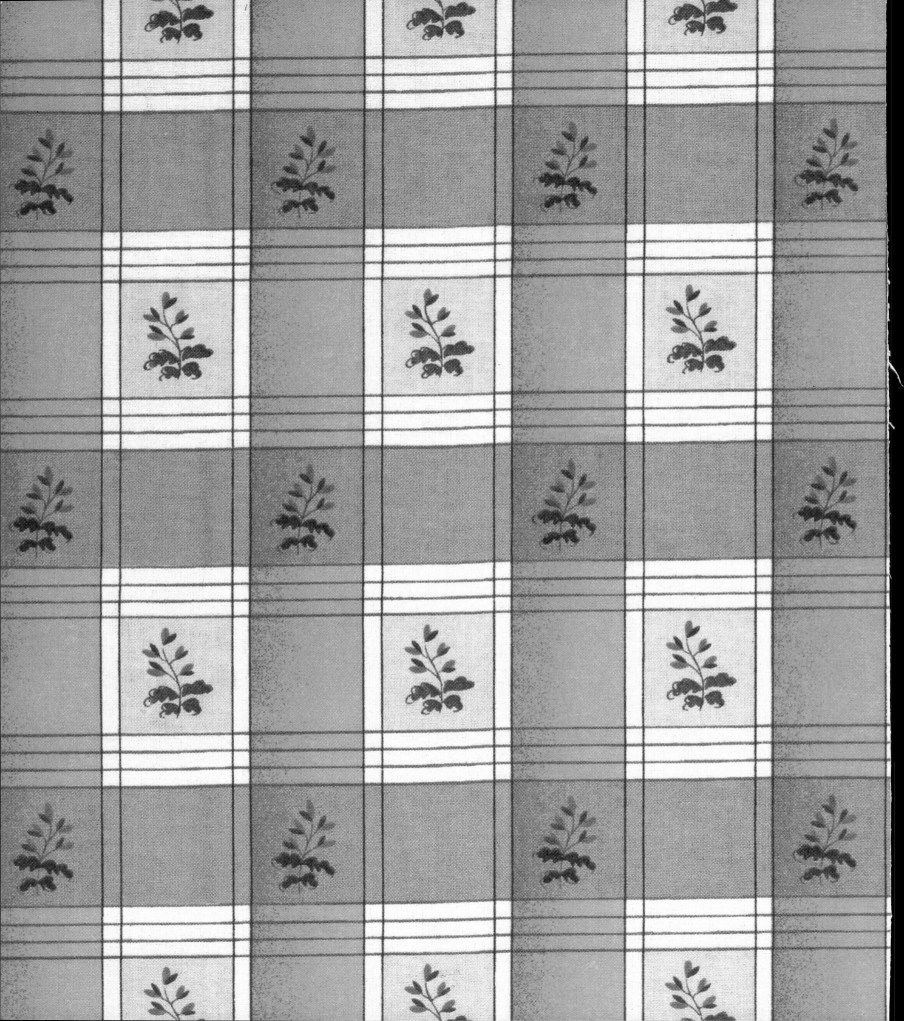

RETAILERS AND DISTRIBUTORS

FABRICS AND WALLPAPERS

UNITED KINGDOM
Nina Campbell furnishing fabrics and wallpapers are distributed by Osborne & Little. They are available at the following retail showrooms:

Nina Campbell Ltd
9 Walton Street, London SW3 2JD.
Tel: 0171 225 1011

Osborne & Little, 304-8 King's Road, London SW3 5UH. Tel: 0171 352 1456

Nina Campbell has a retail concession, selling decorative accessories, at Harvey Nichols, 109-25 Knightsbridge, London SW1X 7RJ.
Tel: 0171 235 5000.

For details of retailers throughout the UK and the Republic of Ireland, contact Osborne & Little Head Office:

Osborne & Little plc, 49 Temperley Road, London SW12 8QE.
Tel: 0181 675 2255

UNITED STATES AND CANADA
For information about Nina Campbell fabrics and wallpapers, contact:

Osborne & Little Head Office
90 Commerce Road,
Stamford, CT 06902.
Tel: 203 359 1500

The following are the main agents for Nina Campbell furnishing fabrics and wallpapers. Their showrooms are open to the trade only.

Atlanta
Ainsworth Noah & Associates Inc., 351 Peachtree Hills Avenue - Suite 518, Atlanta, GA 30305.
Tel: 404 231 8787

Boston
Shechter-Martin, One Design Center Place - Suite 111, Boston, MA 02210.
Tel: 617 951 2526

Chicago
Osborne & Little, Merchandise Mart - Suite 610, Chicago, IL 60654.
Tel: 312 467 0913

Dallas
Boyd Levinson & Company, 1400-C HiLine Drive, Dallas, TX 75207.
Tel: 214 698 0226

Dania
Design West Inc. - DCOTA, 1855 Griffin Road - Suite A-474, Dania, FL 33004. Tel: 305 925 8225 / 8226 / 8227

Denver
Shanavan Collection, Denver Design Center, 595 S. Broadway, Suite 100-S, Denver, CO 80209. Tel: 303 778 7088

Houston
Boyd Levinson & Company, 5120 Woodway - Suite 4001, Houston, TX 77056. Tel: 713 623 2344

Los Angeles
Oakmont, Pacific Design Center - Suite B647, 8687 Melrose Avenue, Los Angeles, CA 90069. Tel: 310 659 1423

Minneapolis
Gene Smiley Showroom, International Market Square, 275 Market Street - Suite 321, Minneapolis, MN 55405.
Tel: 612 332 0402

New York
Osborne & Little Inc., 979 Third Avenue - Suite 520, New York, NY 10022. Tel: 212 751 3333

Philadelpia
JW Showroom Inc., The Marketplace - Suite 304, 2400 Market Street, Philadelphia, PA 19103.
Tel: 215 561 2270

Portland
Stephen E. Earls Showrooms, 2701 N.W. Vaughn - Suite 606, Portland, Oregon 97210.
Tel: 503 227 0541

San Francisco
Randolph & Hein, Galleria Design Center, Suite 101, 101 Henry Adams Street, San Francisco, CA 94103.
Tel: 415 864 3550

Seattle
Stephen E. Earls Showrooms, 520 South Findlay Street, Seattle, WA 98108. Tel: 206 767 7220

Stamford
Osborne & Little Inc., 90 Commerce Road, Stamford, CT 06902.
Tel: 203 359 1500

Washington DC
Osborne & Little Inc., 300 D Street S.W. - Suite 435, Washington, DC 20024. Tel: 202 554 8800

Toronto
Primavera, 160 Pears Avenue - Suite 210, Toronto M5R 1T2, Canada.
Tel: 416 921 3334

REST OF THE WORLD
Worldwide distributors and agents selling Nina Campbell furnishing fabrics and wallpapers:

AUSTRALIA
Wardlaw (Pty) Ltd, 230-232 Auburn Road, Hawthorn, Victoria 3122.
Tel: 03 819 4233

BELGIUM
Donald Thiriar Sprl, Chaussée d'Alsemberg 610, 1180 Brussels.
Tel: 2 3436400

DENMARK
Greengate Interiors,Ordrup Jagtvej 91, 2920 Charlottenlund.
Tel: 39 90 40 01/02

FINLAND
OY SW Lauritzon & Co AB, Elimænkatu 23, SF - 00510 Helsinki.
Tel: 0 1496055

FRANCE
Osborne & Little, 4 rue des Petits Pères, 75002 Paris.
Tel: 1 42 86 91 00

GERMANY
Osborne & Little, Josephspitalstr. 6, 80331 München. Tel: 89 236600

GREECE
Meli SA, 99 Antigonis St, Kolokiathou, 10442 Athens.
Tel: 1 362 7943

ITALY
Donati Remo & C Spa, Corso Tassoni 66, 10144 Torino.
Tel: 11 4376666

JAPAN
Tomita & Co Ltd, 2-3-16 Kyobashi, Chuo-Ku, Tokyo. Tel: 3 3273 7555

LEBANON
Linea Verde, Freeway Building, Sin El-Fil Main Road, PO Box 16, 6174 Beirut. Tel: 1 500 469

NETHERLANDS
Wilhelmine van Aerssen Agenturen, Amsterdamseweg 108-110, 1182 HH Amstelveen.
Tel: 20 640 5060

NEW ZEALAND
Wardlaw (NZ), Cnr Railway & Leek Streets, Newmarket, Auckland 1.
Tel: 9 520 2363

PORTUGAL
Sousa & Holstein, Rua do Patrocínio 128-A, 1350 Lisboa. Tel: 1 3978351

SPAIN
Gaston y Daniela, Hermosilla 26, 28001 Madrid. Tel: 1 4352740

SWEDEN
Cadoro Agenturer AB, Nybrogatan 77, 114 40 Stockholm. Tel: 8 6602346

SWITZERLAND
Ipso Facto, 6 rue Joseph-Girard, CH-1227 Geneva.
Tel: 22 342 5077

TURKEY
Felko AS, Fahri Gizdem Sokak, No 22/1, Gayrettepe 80280, Istanbul.
Tel: 212 266 9921

ROSENTHAL CHINA
Nina Campbell has also produced five exclusive designs for a range of Rosenthal Classic china. For your nearest stockist please contact the following:

AUSTRALIA
Cambur Industries Pty Ltd, 538 Mountain Highway, Bayswater, Melbourne 3153.
Tel: 03 729 5111.

FRANCE
Rosenthal France Sarl, 32, rue de Paradis,F-75010 Paris.
Tel: 1 47709460.

GERMANY
Rosenthal AG,
Wittelsbachstrasse 43,
95100 Selb. Tel: 09287 72 0

GREECE
Ikiakos Exoplismos SA, 47
Agamemnonos Str.,
Kallithea, 17675 Athens.
Tel: 1 9309400

ITALY
Rosenthal Italia Srl, Via Rubattino 4,
I-20134 Milano. Tel: 2 2152241

JAPAN
Takashimaya Trading Co. Ltd, Yoshinobu
Uchida, 2-12-7 Kayabacho, Nihombashi
Chuo-ku, Tokyo 103. Tel: 3 3668 3533

NETHERLANDS
Rosenthal Benelux BV, Porseleinstraat 1,
(Postbus 3703-6202 NS Maastricht), N-
6216 BP Maastricht. Tel: 433 431967

NEW ZEALAND
Accent Distributors Ltd, 475 Mt. Eden
Road, Mt. Eden, Auckland 3.
Tel: 9 638 8082

SPAIN
Dick Import SA, Tomas Redondo, 1,
(Indubuilding-Luarca), 28033 Madrid.
Tel: 1 7642277

SOUTH AFRICA
Spilhaus Silverware Pty. Ltd,
P.O. Box 3265, Cape Town.
Tel: 0027 21 261690

SWEDEN
Rosenthal Skandinavien, Försäljnings
AB, Box 5289, Karlavägen 51, S-
10246, Stockholm. Tel: 8 6605743

UNITED KINGDOM
Rosenthal China (London) Ltd,
Churcham House, 1 Bridgeman Road,
Teddington, Middlesex
TW11 9AJ. Tel: 0181 977 8373.

UNITED STATES
Rosenthal USA Ltd, 355 Michele
Place, Carlstadt, NJ 07072.
Tel: 201 804 8000

*A*CKNOWLEDGMENTS

The author would like to thank: Sally Colvin, Henrietta Konig, Sarah Leather, Claire Leigh, Pippa McGuinness, Jackie McInnes, Kate O'Connor-Fenton, Kathy Prosser and Janine Smith.

The publisher would like to thank the following photographers, artists and organizations for their permission to reproduce the photographs in this book:
5 centre Polly Wreford/Homes & Gardens/Robert Harding Syndication; 7 The Interior Archive/Christopher Simon Sykes; 9 Tim Imrie © House & Garden, The Condé Nast Publications Ltd; 10-11 Derry Moore; 12 The Interior Archive/Fritz von der Schulenburg; 14 The World of Interiors/Fritz von der Schulenburg; 16 Nina Campbell by Osborne & Little; 17 Marianne Topham; 18 below Fritz von der Schulenburg © House & Garden, The Condé Nast Publications Ltd; 19 Fritz von der Schulenburg © House & Garden, The Condé Nast Publications Ltd; 25 The Interior Archive/Fritz von der Schulenburg; 26 The Interior Archive /James Mortimer; 27 Nina Dreyer; 28-9 The Interior Archive/James Mortimer; 30 Nina Dreyer; 32-3 The Interior Archive/Fritz von der Schulenburg; 34 left The Interior Archive/James Mortimer; 34 below Nina Dreyer; 34-35 Window on the World Photo Library/David Usill; 35 right The Interior Archive/James Mortimer; 36 below left The Interior Archive/Christopher Simon Sykes; 36 below right The Interior Archive/James Mortimer; 36 top left The Interior Archive/Fritz von der Schulenburg; 37 Polly Wreford/ Homes & Gardens/Robert Harding Syndication; 38-9 The Interior Archive/James Mortimer; 40 top The Interior Archive/James Mortimer; 40 below The Interior Archive/Fritz von der Schulenburg; 41-51 The Interior Archive/Fritz von der Schulenburg); 97-107 The World of Interiors/James Mortimer; 109-15 John Hall; 144 below P. Chevallier/Madame Figaro; 145 Window on the World Photo Library/David Usill; 146-7 Nina Campbell by Osborne & Little; 147 top right Patrick Van Robaeys/Madame Figaro; 149 Nina Campbell by Osborne & Little; 150 above Nina Campbell by Osborne & Little; 150 below left Nina Dreyer; 150 below right Nina Campbell; 151 Elizabeth Whiting & Associates/Andreas von Einseidel; 154 Pascal Chevalier/Madame Figaro; 155 top World of Interiors/James Mortimer

Every effort has been made to trace copyright holders and we apologize in advance for any unintentional omission and would be pleased to insert appropriate acknowledgment in any subsequent edition of this publication.

The following photographs are courtesy of Nina Campbell:
James Mortimer: 4, 6, 18 left, 21, 22, 39, 53, 54, 55, 56, 57, 58-9, 61, 62, 63, 64, 65, 67, 68, 69, 70, 71, 72, 73 above, 76, 78, 79, 80, 81, 82, 83, 84-5, 86, 87, 90-1, 92, 93, 94-5, 116, 117, 118-9, 120, 121, 122, 123, 124-5, 126, 127, 128, 129, 130, 131, 133, 134, 135, 136, 137, 138, 139, 140, 141, 144 above & left, 148 below, 148 above right, 149 right, 153 below, 155 below.
Paul Chave: 1, 3 (cut-out), 13 ('Ferns' courtesy GP & J Baker Archives), 23, 146 above, 148 above left, 152, 153 above.
Gavin Kingcome: 73 below.

The designs on the following pages (photography by John Richards at Imagepoint, except for page 132 and the endpapers) are by Nina Campbell:
2 Beauly; 3 background Lawn; 4 centre Rockpool; 5 left Queen Bee; 5 right Marot; 8 Coromandel; 24 Sackville Stripe; 42 Meredith; 52 Sir Oliphant; 66 Tulipa; 74 Asticou; 88 Mount Vernon; 96 Artois Stripe; 108 Canton Cargo; 116 Whistler; 132 Famille Rose; 142 & 143 Lord Lyon; 158 Violet Plaid; Endpapers Bumble

The publisher would also like to thank: Alison Bolus, Penny Ford David Lee and Kirsty O'Leary-Leeson.